OUTRAGEOUS WOMEN OF CIVIL WAR TIMES

WITHDRAWN

Mary Rodd Furbee

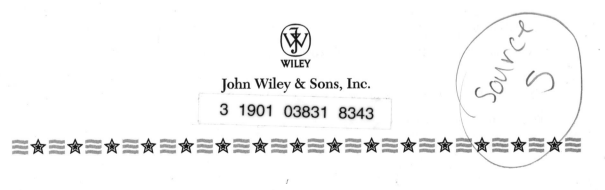

WILEY

John Wiley & Sons, Inc.

This book is printed on acid-free paper. ♾

Copyright © 2003 by Mary Rodd Furbee. All rights reserved

Published by John Wiley & Sons, Inc., Hoboken, New Jersey
Published simultaneously in Canada

Design and production by Navta Associates, Inc.

For general information about our other products and services, please contact our Customer Care Department within the United States at (800) 762-2974, outside the United States at (317) 572-3993 or fax (317) 572-4002.

Wiley also publishes its books in a variety of electronic formats. Some content that appears in print may not be available in electronic books. For more information about Wiley products, visit our web site at www.wiley.com.

Library of Congress Cataloging-in-Publication Data:

Furbee, Mary R. (Mary Rodd), date.
  Outrageous women of Civil War times / Mary Rodd Furbee.
     p. cm.
  Summary: Biographies of some outspoken and influential women of the North and South who broke barriers both in battle and on the home front.
      Contents: Louisa May Alcott—Amelia Bloomer—Susan B. Anthony—Sojourner Truth—Clara Barton—Dorothea Dix—Harriet Tubman—Belle Boyd—Pauline Cushman—Loreta Velazquez—Mary Todd Lincoln—Varina Howell Davis.
  ISBN 0-471-22926-1 (pbk.)
     1. Women—United States—Biography—Juvenile literature. 2. Women—United States—History—19th century—Juvenile literature. 3. United States—History—Civil War, 1861–1865—Juvenile literature. [1. Women—Biography. 2. Women—History—19th century. 3. United States—History—Civil War, 1861–1865.] I. Title.

HQ1412 .F87 2003
920.72'0973'09034—dc21   2002033182

Printed in the United States of America

10 9 8 7 6 5 4 3 2 1

C O N T E N T S

PART FOUR. THE FIRST LADIES

When you picture a Civil War woman, do you see a Southern miss lounging under a magnolia tree surrounded by admirers? Or a prim and proper Northern matron in stiff black silk shuddering over the evils of sin, slavery, and drink?

Before I wrote this book, these were my images of Civil War women, but now I see a far more diverse group of fascinating characters.

I see women who faced down hostile crowds, risked their lives escaping from slavery, and spied against their enemies.

I see women who broke down many barriers to become America's first women nurses, doctors, preachers, professors, and voters.

Most of all, I see women who aimed to change the world—and did.

Between 1840 and 1880, major social changes and a terrible war rocked American society to its foundation. In the North, the population more than doubled and the invention of new machinery transformed industry, modernized farming, and fueled the growth of cities, factories, mills, roads, railroads, and telegraphs. New social groups developed during this period, including very wealthy industrialists; middle-class professionals such as managers, lawyers, doctors, clerks, and bookkeepers; and poorly paid mill and factory workers, many of whom were immigrants from Europe and women.

Gradually, Americans came to accept the notion that it was all right for young single women to be more independent and work outside the home—until they were married, that is. According to law and custom, married women were dependent on (and ruled by) their husbands. In fact, married women could not own property, make decisions about rearing children, sue in court, or sign contracts.

A majority of women did marry and become full-time wives and mothers, for that was still considered the proper role for females. A popular 1830s book, *The Frugal Housewife*, explained why: "Man is daring, confident and great in action; woman in suffering. Man shines abroad, woman at home; man talks to convince, woman to persuade and please."

Most nineteenth-century Americans agreed with this idea, even the famous writer Ralph Waldo Emerson, one of the most modern thinkers of his time. He wrote: "Woman should not write, or fight, or build or compose scores. She does all by inspiring man to do all."

By the 1850s, ideas about women's place in society did change in one important way. Society began to hoist full-time wives and mothers onto a pedestal. The top writers and thinkers of the day praised women as morally superior domestic goddesses. Women had a bit more power in the home (although men still wore the pants—at least until Amelia Bloomer came along!). And they had an all-important duty, to raise brilliant and upstanding sons, and daughters who would become the mothers of such sons.

To carry out their lofty duties, the goddesses began to argue for more education for girls, which before had been limited to elementary school. Suddenly, schools for girls were all the rage. Since these schools needed teachers, star pupils got the jobs. By the end of the nineteenth century, single female teachers dominated a profession that once welcomed only men. (Literacy among women gave us great historical material about the way women lived and thought. As more women learned to read and write, they left behind enough diaries and letters to fill a house.)

Being educated had another impact on women, too. Their eyes were opened to the world beyond their homes, and what they learned dismayed many. The rapid changes in Northern society had given rise to a host of social problems, such as poverty, illiteracy, crime, and alcoholism. Many of the newly educated women began to feel they had a duty to be the moral guardians of society, as well as of their own children. Arm in arm, they emerged from their kitchens and nurseries to set society right again.

At first, these moral reformers were criticized as unnatural for daring to leave their homes. Husbands and fathers fretted that the health of their delicate wives and daughters would be damaged. Yet, despite this criticism and worry, by the 1850s, many middle-class women were devoting themselves to uplifting society.

Most social reformers started by doing charity work among the poor and sick. They fed the hungry, taught English to immigrants, and ran Sunday schools. Yet some daring women, including many featured in this book, soon felt the only long-term solution to society's woes was to tackle the root causes. These women started female reform organizations that worked under the leadership of male-only groups. The antislavery reformers fought to ban slavery (illegal throughout the North) in the South. These abolitionists argued that slavery was immoral and it poisoned all of American society. Meanwhile, temperance advocates saw alcohol abuse as the greatest social evil and worked toward limiting or banning the sale of beer and liquor. Many women reformers advocated both temperance and the abolition of slavery, as well as other humanitarian causes such as better working conditions and wages for factory workers.

Being away from hearth and home was deeply thrilling for many of these former housewives. In fact, they grew confident enough to begin enthusiastically voicing their ideas at conventions attended by delegates from male and female reform organizations. To the women's dismay, however, many male leaders got quite huffy. "It is not proper for women to speak out; you must stay in your place and follow where you are led," the men insisted. In response, a few hundred of the most offended women did just the opposite. In 1848, they organized a convention of their own in Seneca Falls, New York. The 300 delegates to America's first women's rights gathering launched a new movement to win equal opportunities and rights for women.

While daring women in the American North worked, served others, and jumped on the reform wagon, women of the South lived much as their grandmothers had. Unlike the North, the South did not have a thriving middle class of merchants and professionals. (Professionals and merchants, as well as poor whites, lived in the South, but their numbers were small.) Instead, Southern society was divided into two major groups: wealthy, powerful planters and powerless, penniless slaves.

In fact, the major change affecting the South prior to the Civil War was that cotton and tobacco plantations got bigger. Also, because Congress outlawed importing slaves from Africa in 1808, planters did a brisk business breeding and selling slaves. Because of this, planters' wealth and power were completely dependent on the continuation of slavery.

As for the genteel Southern wives and daughters of planters, they sat on pedestals like their Northern sisters. However, the Southern belles were more like frail, captive princesses than goddesses. Their all-powerful husbands and fathers ruled their vast tobacco, sugar, rice, and cotton plantations with iron fists, and they expected their women to be decorative, delicate, and obedient.

Although the Northern and Southern states argued over several issues, it was the debate over slavery in new Western states that finally pushed the nation to war. In the crowded and industrializing North, people hungered for new land and business opportunities. By the hundreds of thousands, they migrated to Western territories, where land was cheap or free. When enough pioneers had settled a Western territory, Congress moved toward making it a new state.

Southern leaders in Congress wanted territories admitted as states that allowed slavery so that they could protect and expand the slave-dependent plantation system. Meanwhile, Northern leaders wanted the new states to be free, which meant no slavery would be allowed.

Early on in the debate, the Missouri Compromise of 1820 had temporarily kept the peace by admitting equal numbers of slave and free states. However, in 1854, the Northern states pushed through the Kansas-Nebraska Act, which let the settlers in the newly created Western states vote on whether to allow slavery. (Far more Northerners than Southerners emigrated to the West, so the South saw this as a serious blow.) One of the major supporters of the bill was Congressman Abraham Lincoln from Illinois.

The debate over slavery progressed, with Lincoln continuing to argue forcefully for limits to slavery, as well as a strong and unified federal government. A few years later, in November 1860, Lincoln was elected president of the United States, even though not one single Southern leader voted for him. Lincoln's victory proved to the proud Southerners that they had become something unthinkable—a powerless minority. Southerners were also convinced that Lincoln's victory sounded a death knell for the institution of slavery.

Unable to accept either one of those realities, South Carolina left the Union in 1861. Mississippi, Florida, Alabama, Georgia, Louisiana, and Texas (in that order) soon followed. The rebel states formed the Confederate States of America (or Confederacy for short) and elected Jefferson Davis president.

Both the North and the South quickly raised armies, and the Confederacy began to seize U.S. property. On April 12, 1861, Confederate soldiers under General P. G. T. Beauregard successfully bombarded and took over Fort Sumter, off the coast of Charleston, South Carolina; then Virginia, Arkansas, North Carolina, and Tennessee seceded and joined the Confederacy. (Several border states that allowed slavery stayed with the Union: Maryland, Kentucky, Delaware, and Missouri. But roughly half of the families in the border states had such strong economic and cultural ties to the South that their sons fought with the Confederacy. In fact, in some families, some sons wore blue and others wore gray.)

No one predicted the terrible price the nation would pay for this war that pitted American against American. It was the first modern war fought with weapons capable of killing and maiming many. More than 600,000 soldiers died—more than all deaths from all American wars combined—and 500,000 more were wounded. About 60 women serving on the battlefield, either in disguise or serving as nurses or flag bearers, also died.

After initial victories by the Confederacy, the larger, better-supplied Union finally won the war. Abraham Lincoln's issuing of the Emancipation Proclamation, signed on January 1, 1863, which officially freed the slaves, also helped defeat the South. All over the South, most of the 4 million newly freed slaves put down their hoes and brooms and hiked to the nearest Union Army encampment for protection. Behind them, planters' cotton and tobacco died in the fields. On April 9, 1865, four years after the war began, the Confederacy surrendered at Appomattox Court House in Virginia.

You've probably read a great deal about the battles and the generals of the bloody Civil War. But you may not know that more than 400 women disguised themselves as men and fought in battle. Also, between 4,000 and 6,000 women worked as military nurses, and one determined female doctor worked as a Union Army surgeon. Thousands of women raised funds for both the Union and Confederate armies, too, and worked as cooks, laundresses, and color guards. Some, including a couple of amazing women you'll meet in this book, even served as spies.

Although Southern women were more restricted than their Northern sisters, they coped heroically with food shortages, and several faced down social disapproval to become nurses.

Meanwhile, black women in the South escaped slavery on the Underground Railroad. Some also worked as cooks for the 25th Army Corps, America's first all-black infantry regiments. And black women who could read and write taught in freedman's schools for black children, soldiers, and other adults.

Women of the Civil War era were survivors, pioneers, and trailblazers. They helped the needy, hid secret messages in their hoop skirts, lobbied Congress against unjust laws, and braved the battlefield. They fearlessly defied tyranny and devoted their lives to helping and liberating others. Against great odds, they proved that strong and determined women can change the world for the better.

Part One

REFORMERS
AND WRITERS

Louisa May Alcott

(1 8 3 2 – 1 8 8 8)

When Louisa May Alcott was a child, a sign above her family's front door read: "True genius is infinite patience." Yet Louisa, the genius of the brainy Alcott clan, had far more passion and ambition than patience. Rather than "denying her selfish desires," as she'd been taught, Louisa dreamed of an independent life as a successful career woman. With great determination, she realized that dream, and today we know her as one of America's most respected authors.

Born in 1832 to Bronson and Abba Alcott, Louisa May Alcott spent her early years in Boston, then in 1840 moved with her family to Concord, Massachusetts. She and her three younger sisters—Anna, Elizabeth, and May—were much loved (although her parents spent a lot of time trying to "tame" the rambunctious Louisa).

The Alcotts belonged to an intellectual group of leading New England writers, thinkers, and teachers known as the Transcendentalists. While most Christians saw human beings as sinners who had to strive to be good and therefore find salvation, Transcendentalists had a different philosophy. They wanted to explore and discover new truths about God,

Many of Louisa's neighbors were leading Transcendentalists, such as the great American literary figure Henry David Thoreau. Thoreau left "civilization" to live a primitive life close to nature—something the Alcotts would experiment with, too. In a little cabin by a pond, Thoreau wrote about getting in touch with nature and himself, in a famous book called *On Walden Pond.* The pond was on the property of another Transcendentalist neighbor of the Alcotts, the author Ralph Waldo Emerson. He let Louisa use his private library whenever she liked, and he published the Transcendentalist magazine *The Dial.* Louisa's father wrote for this publication.

science, and humankind. They believed in a higher power, but not in churches that interpreted and laid down religious laws. They believed individuals should use their instincts and rational thought to decide what was right and wrong.

The Alcotts' unconventional beliefs exposed Louisa to well-known intellectuals of the day and allowed Louisa and her sisters to have a magical childhood. While other middle-class children memorized verses in stuffy classrooms (students mostly memorized facts and rarely discussed ideas), Bronson Alcott taught his daughters at home. Later in life, Louisa recalled morning lessons: "My father taught in the wise way which unfolds what lies in the child's nature as a flower blooms, rather than crammed it, like a Strasburg goose. I never liked arithmetic nor grammar, but reading, writing, composition, history, and geography I enjoyed, as well as the stories read to us with a skill peculiarly his own."

Unfortunately, many parents with school-aged children did not agree with Bronson Alcott's views about education, which included his insistence that boys and girls, and blacks and whites, be taught together. These ideas were so strange to even the most advanced thinkers of the day that Bronson had a hard time earning enough to support his family.

In schools he founded himself or where he was hired to teach, irate parents were always withdrawing students or insisting that Bronson be fired.

Because of Bronson's on-again, off-again teaching career, the family often struggled financially. But no matter how empty the Alcott cupboard was, Abba always found something to pack into baskets for those who were worse off. Only after Louisa and her sisters did their lessons and made their charitable rounds were they allowed to scamper off and play.

But what play it was! While other "respectable" girls sat in stuffy, dusty parlors doing needlepoint, the Alcott girls were free to romp about unsupervised (to the horror and dismay of some neighbors). Sometimes, when Louisa was small, she tended to take her freedom too far and wandered off alone without a word to anyone. One day, she headed for the town ash heap to play with the children of some poor Irish immigrants. Louisa's sisters found her covered in soot, chowing down on salt fish and potatoes. Another time, Louisa was found conked out in the doorway of a village store curled up with a big shaggy dog. Sometimes, Louisa also crept into her father's study, which was strictly forbidden. There she lost herself in books of fairy tales, and, even worse, drew pictures of elves and fairies in the margins!

Despite her own best efforts, Louisa never was able to govern her passions. As she grew older, she grew bolder, leading her sisters and a group of local ragamuffins on romps through the countryside around Concord. They picked berries, played at being fairies, and ran races through the meadows. Daredevil Louisa May ran full tilt, too, faster than any boy or girl in the village.

Before she hit her teen years, Louisa began writing. She wrote, directed, and starred in plays based on fairy tales and William Shakespeare's works. In a neighbor's barn, the Alcott girls hung tablecloths for curtains and cobbled together props from kitchen utensils. Louisa played the lead villain, whether it was a king, queen, pirate, ghost, or bandit. And she always stole the show. "Our giant came tumbling off a loft, when Jack cut down the squash-vine running up a ladder to represent that immortal bean," she later wrote. "Cinderella rolled away in a vast pumpkin, and elves held their pretty revels among the pines. Flying ladies came swinging down on the birch tree-tops, lords and ladies haunted the garden, and mermaids splashed in the bath-house of woven willows over the brook."

In 1843, when Louisa was 11, Bronson Alcott was tired of trying to remain true to his ideals in a world that didn't understand or accept them. He decided it was time for the Alcott family to truly live the Transcendentalist philosophy—to live simply, close to nature. With several other utopians—people who created "ideal" communities of like-minded souls—Bronson hoped to create a Garden of Eden on earth.

Bronson's friend from England, Charles Lane, put up the money to buy a 90-acre farm near Harvard University. Seven men and one woman joined Bronson, Abba, and the Alcott girls at the farm. The adults promised to share equally in the work and not to depend on the outside world for anything. This meant they had to cut their own wood, sew their own clothes, teach their own children, and grow all their own fruit and vegetables. (The group raised no livestock, for they considered animals too difficult to raise and meat unhealthy.) Because they planned to live off the "fruits of the earth," the group named the farm Fruitlands. Years later, in 1873, Louisa would write a humorous book about the experience titled *Transcendental Wild Oats*.

Although Louisa's father was all fired up about communal living, trying to live off the land wore Louisa's mother and the girls to a frazzle. They didn't mind not eating meat, but they sure missed their coffee, tea, molasses, milk, butter, and eggs! Plus there wasn't much of anything to eat because the men were horrid farmers. They planted seeds at the wrong time and the crops failed. They pruned orchard trees with the wrong tools and killed all the trees. Meanwhile, Abba Alcott, her girls, and the other adult woman, Ann Page, struggled to feed the little group.

After only seven months, Bronson Alcott and the others were forced to admit their experiment had failed. The family moved back to Concord and settled in for good. At first the family lived in a house called Hillside, bought with money Abba inherited. Later, in 1857, the family moved to Orchard House, which today is a museum devoted to Louisa May Alcott and her family.

TRANSCENDENTAL WILD OATS

The excerpt below from *Transcendental Wild Oats* is based on a true story about Ann Page (named Jane in the book). She was the commune's only female resident besides Abba Alcott (called Mrs. Lamb) and her girls. "Beasts of burden" means horses or oxen that could haul things.

Sleep, food, and poetic musings were the desires of dear Jane's life, and she shirked all duties as clogs upon her spirit's wings. Any thought of lending a hand with the domestic drudgery never occurred to her; and when to the question, "Are there any beasts of burden on the place?" Mrs. Lamb answered, with a face that told its own tale, "Only one woman!" The buxom Jane took no shame to herself, but laughed at the joke, and let the stout-hearted sister tug on alone. Unfortunately, the poor lady hankered after the flesh-pots, and endeavored to stay herself with private sips of milk, crackers, and cheese, and on one dire occasion she partook of fish at a neighbor's table. One of the children reported this sad lapse from virtue, and poor Jane was publicly reprimanded by Timon.

"I only took a little bit of the tail," sobbed the penitent poetess.

"Yes, but the whole fish had to be tortured and slain that you might tempt your carnal appetite with that one taste of the tail. Know ye not, consumers of flesh meat, that ye are nourishing the wolf and tiger in your bosoms?"

At this awful question and the peal of laughter which arose from some of the younger brethren, tickled by the ludicrous contrast between the stout sinner, the stern judge, and the naughty satisfaction of the young detective, poor Jane fled from the room to pack her trunk and return to the world where fishes' tails were not forbidden fruit.

Although communal life was behind them, the Alcotts' hard times were hardly over. The family had sunk all its savings into Fruitlands, and Bronson was without a job. To try and restore the family finances, Bronson Alcott went on a lecture tour. Abba Alcott also entered the job market, doing social work among new immigrants to America.

Louisa deeply admired and respected her mother, and it's easy to see why. Along with working to put food on the table, Abba helped run an antislavery group, helped the local poor, and kept the household running smoothly. Sometimes Louisa felt she should try to be just like her saintly mother, but that was impossible. Abba Alcott was patient, gentle, and brought up in a time when women always put their families first. Louisa, however, was spirited, ambitious, and lived in a time when determined women were breaking new ground. In fact, Louisa was quite angry about the obstacles faced by women who wanted to have professions.

"I am angry nearly every day of my life," she wrote in her diary, "especially about being a useless girl, untrained in any profession. But I will do something by and by. I don't care what—teach, sew, act, write—anything to help the family. I'll be rich and famous and happy before I die, see if I won't."

After the Fruitlands failure, 12-year-old Louisa launched her first effort at earning money to help her family. She hung a handwritten sign in the family's front window—"Louisa May Alcott, Doll Dressmaker"—and neighborhood children flocked to the little shop. It was only a brief success, however, because Louisa wasn't at all fond of playing with dolls and she didn't care for sewing! Other of Louisa's enthusiasms led to more short-lived money-making schemes, such as reading to an elderly man and doing laundry.

Although determined to earn money, Louisa found society's limited options for women very frustrating. But giving up wasn't an option: "I'll make a battering-ram of my head and make my way through this rough and tumble world," she wrote.

Louisa's most heartfelt dreams were to become either an actress or a writer, but her parents discouraged both. Professional acting was far less respectable than amateur dramatics, and the Alcotts shared to some extent the widely held belief that only vain, unladylike women would perform in public. As for Louisa becoming a professional writer, the Alcotts probably didn't want Louisa to have to walk such a difficult path. Female writers had to use male pen names or initials of their first names to disguise their sex and shield themselves against prejudice.

Instead of acting or writing, Louisa's parents steered her in a practical direction. They suggested a steady and admirable profession only recently opened to single women: teaching. At 17, Louisa took her first teaching job, and with her earnings she helped ease her family's poverty. For several years she did her best to do a good job. Try as she might, though, Louisa couldn't damp down her need to write. So every day after school, she churned out stacks of romantic stories and novels. "Far away there in the sunshine are my highest aspirations," the ever hopeful Louisa wrote. "I may not reach them, but I can look up and see their beauty, believe in them, and try to follow where they lead."

When Louisa was 19, a magazine bought her first poem, and several published short stories followed. Like other women writers, she published anonymously or used a pen name. But by age 22, Louisa had grown confident enough to quit teaching, move to Boston to live on her own, and publish a book under her own name. *Flower Fables* by Louisa May Alcott was a charming book about the origins of the names of flowers, and it sold quite well. It didn't, however, bring Louisa the respect she craved. Even her own publisher was still saying, "Louisa, my dear, it really would be best if you give up writing and go back to teaching." Thankfully, Louisa didn't take such advice to heart. "I am not afraid of storms," she wrote, "for I am learning how to sail my ship."

Louisa's version of sailing her own ship meant trying her hand at writing some "blood and thunder" tales of romance and adventure. She also rekindled her interest in drama by attending Boston theaters, and she joined the antislavery movement. One close ally and friend was Julia Ward Howe, who wrote the Union anthem, *The Battle Hymn of the Republic.*

Sadly, family duties soon ended Louisa's brief, joyously independent life. In 1857, the death of her sister Elizabeth, then the marriage of her sister Anna, left Louisa with the responsibility of caring for her parents as they grew older. Louisa returned to live with them at Orchard House in Concord.

That didn't mean Louisa stopped writing, though, and her greatest successes were yet to come. Under the name A. M. Barnard, Louisa found publishers for her romantic thrillers and wrote many more. In stories such as "A Long Fatal Love Chase" and "Pauline's Passion and Punishment," Louisa featured fallen actresses and despised divorcées who were mistreated by society. Yet unlike other romances of the day, Louisa's fallen women characters had hearts of gold. Instead of being doomed in the end, they found happiness, respect, or fame. Louisa's work sold like hotcakes, and she continued to support her parents, as she would for the rest of her life.

The Civil War ushered in a new phase in Louisa's life. Like her parents, Louisa viewed the war as a holy battle to free the slaves. In 1859, when the militant abolitionist John Brown tried to steal weapons and arm slaves so that they would revolt, Louisa was sympathetic. Before and during the conflict, her family harbored many fugitive slaves at Orchard House.

Yet such contributions didn't feel like nearly enough to passionate Louisa, who threw herself down on her bed and wept because she was female and could not be a soldier in the Union Army. Instead, Louisa did the next best thing. On her 30th birthday in 1862, she applied to become a nurse for the newly formed U.S. Sanitary Commission.

"Decided to go to Washington as a nurse if I could find a place," she wrote in her diary in the fall of 1862. "Help needed, and I love nursing, and must let out my pent up energy in some new way. I want new experiences, and am sure to get 'em if I go. So I've sent in my name."

In the past, military nursing had been done by the soldiers' wives who

DEADLY DISEASES OF THE NINETEENTH CENTURY

During the Civil War, disease took a greater toll than bullets. More than 16,000 doctors, assistants, and nurses treated 250,000 wounds—and 7 million cases of disease. Historians estimate that only one-third of the 600,000 Civil War deaths stemmed from warfare itself. The remaining two-thirds were from disease. Hundreds of the 4,000 to 6,000 women who served as Civil War nurses also caught diseases, and dozens died (exact numbers are hard to determine). In those days, doctors knew little about how germs, poor diets, and bad sanitation in overcrowded camps contributed to deaths from disease. Antibiotics didn't exist and some of the medicines doctors tried (like mercury) actually poisoned patients. Typhoid, one of the biggest killers, was brought on by drinking contaminated water and milk. Other common and deadly diseases included cholera, dysentery, lung fever, malaria, scarlet fever, smallpox, and yellow fever.

traveled with the troops, and wounded soldiers who were on the mend. But for this large-scale, modern war, Dorothea Dix (see chapter 6) helped convince the federal government to create a corps of paid nurses. Only one in ten applicants was hired, and Louisa was among them.

At Union Hotel Hospital in the nation's capital, Louisa became a nurse and helped care for 400 sick and dying men. It was exhausting work, but Louisa found it rewarding. "I started on my long journey, full of hope and sorrow, courage and plans," she entered into her diary. "A most interesting journey, into a new world full of stirring sights and sounds, new adventures, and an ever-growing sense of the great task I had undertaken. I said my prayers as I went rushing through the country with white tents, all alive with patriotism, and already red with blood. A solemn time, but I'm glad to live in it; and I am sure it will do me good, whether I come out alive or dead."

In the hospital, Louisa dressed wounds, soothed fevered brows, and helped soldiers write letters to their sweethearts. As long as she was needed, Louisa planned to continue her work as a nurse. But like many patients and many nurses, Louisa caught typhoid fever. After only a few months, she had to abandon her wartime nursing career and go home to Concord to recuperate. Although Louisa fought off the typhoid, mercury in the medicine she was given poisoned her, and from that she never fully recovered.

Louisa was supposed to rest, but she was incapable of putting down her pen. While her wartime experience was fresh in her mind, she wrote a book called *Hospital Sketches.* Louisa painted a realistic and moving portrait of the Civil War doctors, nurses, and soldiers. Everyone in the book had fictional names (a common practice at the time), and Louisa was Tribulation Periwinkle. Dorothea Dix was called Florence Nightingale, after the famous European nurse who had started the first army nursing corps in the world.

☆≋☆≋☆≋☆≋☆≋☆≋☆≋☆≋☆≋☆≋☆≋☆≋☆≋☆≋☆≋☆≋

FROM *HOSPITAL SKETCHES,* 1863

Having been run over by three excited surgeons, bumped against by water-pails, and small boys, nearly scalded by an avalanche of newly-filled tea-pots, and hopelessly entangled in a knot of colored sisters coming to wash, I progressed by slow stages up stairs and down, till the main hall was reached, and I paused to take breath and a survey. . . . The sight of several stretchers, each with its legless, armless, or desperately wounded occupant, entering my ward, admonished me that I was there to work, not to wonder or weep; so I corked up my feelings, and returned to the path of duty, which was rather "a hard road to travel" just then. . . . Round the great stove was gathered the dreariest group I ever saw—ragged, gaunt and pale, mud to the knees, with bloody bandages untouched since put on days before; many bundled up in blankets, coats being lost or useless; and all wearing that disheartened look which proclaimed defeat. . . . I pitied them so much. . . . I yearned to serve the dreariest of them all.

☆≋☆≋☆≋☆≋☆≋☆≋☆≋☆≋☆≋☆≋☆≋☆≋☆≋☆≋☆≋☆≋

THE PUBLICATION
OF *LITTLE WOMEN*
MADE LOUISA A
LITERARY STAR.

Louisa wrote *Hospital Sketches* under her own name, and when it became a bestseller, she at last became a known and respected literary figure. A job writing and editing a children's magazine called *Merry's Museum* also helped her career, for the publisher, Thomas Niles, encouraged Louisa to write a children's novel. Louisa did just that, and in 1868, the novel *Little Women* transformed her from a literary name to a literary star!

The children's novel about the fictional March family in Concord, Massachusetts, sold a million copies—and it has been a bestseller ever since. Louisa's own family and childhood provided material for the book, with the character Josephine (or Jo) standing in for Louisa herself. The character Beth was much like Louisa's musical sister, Elizabeth, who died at age 22 from scarlet fever. The character Amy was based on Louisa's artistic sister, May. And the character Meg resembled Louisa's sister Anna. Several sequels about the March family soon followed, including *Little Men* (1871) and *Jo's Boys* (1886). Louisa also published *Work* in 1873, *Eight Cousins* in 1874, and *Rose in Bloom* in 1876.

Although based on her family, Louisa's work was still fiction. She sweetened her memories to create a rosy picture of family life because that's what she believed readers wanted. For example, as the heroine of *Little Women,* Jo was a live wire, just as Louisa had been. In the end, however, the fictional Jo lived a far more conventional life than the real Louisa did. While Jo settled down, got married, and had children, such a life never entered into Louisa's dreams. "Work," she wrote in her diary, "is my salvation."

During these years when her career took off, Louisa also worked for women's suffrage, and in 1879 she was the first Concord woman to reg-

ister to vote in a school board election. However, Louisa was way too busy working and caring for her parents to devote very much time to causes. Once a feminist friend foolishly suggested to Louisa that she should do more, and Louisa understandably shot back, "I'm just a bit too busy proving Woman's Right to Labor, to help gain the Woman's Right to Vote!"

Declining health, as a result of the mercury that was slowly poisoning her system, also left Louisa with little steam for anything but family and her writing career. After 1879, a new responsibility came along that took up even more of her energies. That year, May Alcott, Louisa's sister, died suddenly, leaving 6-week-old Louisa May (Lulu) for Louisa to raise. After that, many of the wonderful stories that flowed from Louisa's pen were especially for her adored niece. These were published as *Lulu's Library*.

In 1885, Louisa, her parents, and Lulu moved to an elegant home in Boston's Louisburg Square. Three years later, in 1888, Louisa nursed her ailing father until his death. On his deathbed, Bronson Alcott said to Louisa, "I am going up. Come with me." And Louisa, who didn't fear death at all, replied, "Oh, I wish I could." Louisa's father died on March 4, and two days later, Louisa collapsed and died, too. She is buried in Concord's Sleepy Hollow Cemetery, on a ridge where Ralph Waldo Emerson, Nathaniel Hawthorne, and Henry David Thoreau are also buried.

In death, as in life, Louisa May Alcott joined the ranks of America's finest literary stars.

Amelia Bloomer

(1 8 1 8 – 1 8 9 4)

W omen's long, heavy skirts have made us unpaid street sweepers long enough," Amelia Bloomer wrote in her 1850s magazine, *The Lily*. A fashion revolution was needed, she preached, and so was a social revolution that gave women equal rights with men.

Amelia's parents, Ananias and Lucy Jenks, may not have been surprised that Amelia grew up to insist that women could literally wear the pants in the family (along with men). After all, the Jenks family ran a clothing store in Homer, New York. The Jenks also raised five children to have a deep faith in God (they were Presbyterians) and strong principles about what was right and wrong.

Amelia, born in 1818, was said to be a quiet, cheerful, and very smart child—so smart, in fact, that even though she only attended school for two years, as a teenager she began to teach school herself. Love cut short that career, however, for when Amelia was 22, she fell for the Quaker newspaper editor Dexter Bloomer of Seneca Falls. Although Quakers frowned on marrying outside the faith, Dexter was a bit of a rebel, as was Amelia. The couple married in 1840—and at the ceremony, Amelia did not promise to "obey" her husband, as was common then.

Despite that bold beginning to married life, the young couple led a quiet existence for several years. Amelia cheerfully kept house, raised two children, and was active in the local temperance society. She also wrote articles denouncing the "demon drink" for her husband's newspaper.

In 1848, Amelia's life changed dramatically after a group of earnest women descended on Seneca Falls for America's first women's rights convention. The Quaker leader Lucretia Mott and Susan B. Anthony (see chapter 3) organized the conference because the male-dominated reform movements refused to let them and other women speak in public or hold leadership positions.

Curiosity led Amelia to attend as an observer, and at first she thought the black-clad women were terribly serious and intense. To the cheerful Amelia it seemed that the women had pretty comfortable lives, and she didn't understand why they weren't satisfied. Yet as she watched from

☆≡☆≡☆≡☆≡☆≡☆≡☆≡☆≡☆≡☆≡☆≡☆≡☆≡☆≡☆≡☆≡

THE TEMPERANCE MOVEMENT

In the early 1800s, the number of men who drank alcohol—and too much of it—had skyrocketed. Most likely, rapid social change was to blame. In those days, in a single year, Americans drank an average of 7 gallons of pure alcohol—also called bark juice, tar water, old red eye, or oh-be-joyful.

In response to this trend, Protestant churches launched the temperance movement, which pushed for limiting, regulating, or even banning the sale of alcohol. Temperance supporters believed that drinking led to damnation. They also felt that alcohol abuse was the root cause of most social problems, including poverty, unemployment, and crime.

The first temperance groups were small, all male, and church affiliated. Then in the 1830s and 1840s, masses of women got involved. During the Civil War, the movement petered out as Northern reformers concentrated on other issues, such as fighting slavery, winning rights for women, and the war itself. After the war, however, the movement reemerged and grew by leaps and bounds. By the century's end, a group called the Women's Christian Temperance Union had chapters in almost every city and small town in America.

☆≡☆≡☆≡☆≡☆≡☆≡☆≡☆≡☆≡☆≡☆≡☆≡☆≡☆≡☆≡☆≡

the sidelines, Amelia kept an open mind. She listened to discussions by the 300 delegates to the Convention to Discuss the Social, Civil, and Religious Condition of Women. She listened carefully to the reading of "The Declaration of Sentiments," which about a hundred delegates signed. She listened as the Seneca Falls delegates discussed why women had no rights to the estates of their husbands and why women could not get custody of their children if a couple separated.

At the historic convention, the speakers also lamented that few colleges admitted women and that women were restricted to being mothers and wives. The most daring of the bunch even suggested that it was "the duty of the women of this country to secure to themselves their sacred right to the elective franchise [the right to vote]." And the applause was deafening as the fired-up delegates swore to "employ agents, circulate tracts, petition the State and national Legislatures, and endeavor to enlist the pulpit and the press in our behalf."

FROM "THE DECLARATION OF SENTIMENTS," 1848

The history of mankind is a history of repeated injuries and usurpations on the part of man toward woman, having in direct object the establishment of an absolute tyranny over her. To prove this, let facts be submitted to a candid world. He has never permitted her to exercise her inalienable right to the elective franchise [the vote]. He has compelled her to submit to laws, in the formation of which she had no voice. He has withheld from her rights which are given to the most ignorant and degraded men—both natives and foreigners. . . . He has made her, if married, in the eye of the law, civilly dead. He has taken from her all right in property, even to the wages she earns. He has made her, morally, an irresponsible being, as she can commit many crimes, with impunity, provided they be done in the presence of her husband. In the covenant of marriage, she is compelled to promise obedience to her husband, he becoming, to all intents and purposes, her master—the law giving him power to deprive her of her liberty.

After the convention, Amelia went home to let these new ideas simmer a while and to read the press accounts of the convention. There were many of those, too, for the convention raised a great hue and cry. Editors and public leaders blasted America's first women's rights advocates as "bitter old maids and divorcées" and "the shrieking sisterhood." Some even accused the women of having been under the influence of drink when they signed the declaration!

Of course, Amelia realized how ridiculous it was to accuse the highly proper, teetotaling women of being tipsy. She found the other put-downs offensive, too. That, plus the new ideas bubbling in her brain, gave her a host of insights. Everywhere Amelia looked, she saw men who weren't nearly as supportive and respectful as her own husband. Many men allowed the women in their families no say in how to raise their own children or spend their own money. And some ministers even insisted women had no souls, which was why they needed to be ruled by men.

The more Amelia thought about it, the more she realized that the Seneca Falls women were on to something big. It began to dawn on her that she, too, had untapped talents and ambitions. She wanted to write and publish more. She wanted to help change the world. Within only a year of the Seneca Falls convention, Amelia took up the banner of the women's rights movement. Then, not content to just go to meetings and conventions, she founded a women's magazine—the first ever published by an American woman.

The Lily, Amelia's twice-weekly publication, was a hit. In fact, her editorial recipe for success still guides many women's magazines today. Amelia

AMELIA'S MAGAZINE FEATURED FASHIONS, HOUSEHOLD TIPS, AND CALLS FOR WOMEN TO STAND UP FOR THEIR RIGHTS.

THE LILY.

DEVOTED TO THE INTERESTS OF WOMAN.

AMELIA BLOOMER,   EDITOR AND PUBLISHER.

GODEY'S LADY'S BOOK

Sarah Hale edited and managed *Godey's Lady's Book*, America's first popular women's magazine. (Unlike Amelia, Sarah didn't own the magazine, a man named Godey did.) *Godey's* offered health tips, recipes, sheet music, book reviews, and fashion spreads, along with essays and short stories that stressed women's moral and domestic duties. Sarah Hale, unlike Amelia, did not advocate women's rights or suffrage in the pages of *Godey's*. She did, however, push for women's schools and colleges. In 1846, Sarah wrote, "The time of action is now. We must redeem woman from her inferior position and place her side by side with man, a help-mate for him in all his pursuits."

realized that many women were just like her. They wanted information about domestic things—sewing, cooking, child rearing, dress patterns, and household budgets. Yet they were also interested in voting, higher education for women, wage equality, and marriage laws.

Although Amelia's magazine struck a chord with American women, she would never have become a household name if she hadn't caught sight of her cousin wearing a pair of baggy pants gathered at the bottom. Elizabeth Smith Miller came to visit wearing pouffy trousers she'd bought while on a tour of Europe. The pouffy pants were covered to just below the knees with a wide, gathered shirt. The outfit delighted Amelia, for it didn't restrict women like the heavy, bulky clothes of the day.

Fashionable women of Amelia's time were draped from head to toe in layers of wire and bone corsets, hoops, petticoats, and long, heavy skirts. In 1800, dresses only weighed about 8 ounces, but by 1840 they weighed from 8 to 16 pounds! Men insisted women fainted because they were frail, but it was all that scrunching and weight that left them gasping for air. Nothing about this getup was comfortable or practical. In fact, fashion sometimes got positively silly. For example, the 1870s bustle replaced hoops. The bustle, a spring covered with horsehair, was worn over rear ends to enlarge women's hips.

Inspired, Amelia ditched all her layers and flounces, donned the new costume, then sang its praises in *The Lily*. The fabric was light as a feather and loose-fitting, she told readers. Not a bit of skin showed, either, so it was "modest" and "decent" enough for a proper lady.

All over America, a handful of daring women also began wearing the trousers, and because Amelia pushed them, everyone soon called them bloomers. Believe it or not, this set off a huge hullabaloo! People on the streets jeered and hissed at Amelia and other bloomer wearers. "The petticoat is sacred," ministers preached. "Men will ogle your plump legs," husbands complained to wives. Of course, it wasn't really the bloomers people feared; it was what they represented. Women were supposed to be beautiful and weak. Men, the lords and masters, were supposed to wear the pants in the family. If women wanted to wear pants, it meant they wanted power (which they did!).

In response to this criticism, Amelia became a fashion revolutionary. Bloomers were no longer just practical; they were a way to declare independence from tyranny. "You won't be free until you crush your corsets," she cheered in *The Lily* and in speeches she gave about fashion reform

☆≋☆≋☆≋☆≋☆≋☆≋☆≋☆≋☆≋☆≋☆≋☆≋☆≋☆≋☆≋

THE SOLDIER AND THE SKIRT

Tales abound of wartime women smugglers hiding medicine, food, messages, ammunition, and love letters under their sizable skirts. But—hiding a man? During the war, a Rochester, New York, newspaper told of a young boy who enlisted in the U.S. Army. After a short while, the boy ditched army life and deserted, but a guard captured him. On the way back to camp, during a stopover at a saloon, the deserter escaped. He ran into the kitchen, and when the guard dashed after him, he'd completely vanished. Later the tavern's cook admitted that she had hid the deserter under her wide skirt!

☆≋☆≋☆≋☆≋☆≋☆≋☆≋☆≋☆≋☆≋☆≋☆≋☆≋☆≋☆≋

and women's rights. "Let there be no stain of earth upon your dress or your soul—quit groveling in the dirt!"

Yet despite Amelia's best efforts, bloomers did not revolutionize fashion—or liberate women. American society just wasn't ready for women in pants, and those who wore them decided that being considered freakish didn't help with winning converts to their ways of thinking. So after a few short years, Amelia and other bloomer wearers went back to their long, heavy skirts.

With her bloomers gathering dust in the closet, Amelia once again looked like a respectable matron. But on the inside she hadn't changed a bit. In 1855, she moved with her husband to the wilds of Council Bluffs, Iowa, where she organized the women into Soldiers' Aid societies and reform groups.

Before Amelia's death in 1894, a bloomer revival hit the younger generation, who wore the pantaloons for swimming and bicycling. Amelia Bloomer lived long enough to see women in pants that bore her name happily splashing about in the surf and whirling about town. The fashion revolution, begun by Amelia Bloomer, was in full swing.

THE VIVANDIÈRES

Some women who traveled with both the Union and Confederate troops wore bloomers—and never got ribbed for it! *Vivandières* (a French word meaning "givers of hospitality") served as regimental flag bearers. The practice stemmed from a European tradition, and the young women were usually daughters or wives of officers. The Vivandières wore short jackets modeled after the regiment's uniforms and bright silk or velvet skirts over bloomer pants. Most marched only in parades, but some marched into battle, too. Mary Tepe of Pennsylvania earned a decoration for bravery after being wounded in Fredericksburg. Kady Brownell of Rhode Island came under heavy fire at the Battle of Bull Run and was honored in a poem called *Kady Brownell: The Daughter of the Regiment* by Clinton Scollard.

CHAPTER 3

Susan B. Anthony

(1820–1906)

When the women's rights crusader Susan B. Anthony spoke before audiences, hecklers sometimes threw rotten eggs at her and shouted things like "Home wrecker!" Susan always stayed cool as a cucumber, though, for deep in her heart she believed that failure was impossible.

Susan Anthony, born in 1820 in Adams, Massachusetts, was the second of Daniel and Lucy Anthony's eight children. When Susan was 6, her father got a job managing a cotton mill in Battenville, New York, and the family moved to a large house nearby. The Anthonys needed lots of space, for along with eight children, a half-dozen mill workers (daughters of local farmers) boarded with them on weeknights.

ELIZABETH CADY STANTON (LEFT) AND SUSAN B. ANTHONY (RIGHT).

In the Anthonys' Quaker household, Susan learned early that the way to honor God was to work hard and serve others. Susan also learned that it was her duty to always resist tyranny. "Put your foot down where you mean to stand, and let no one move you from the right," her father taught.

Like many Quakers, Susan's parents also approved of schooling for girls, so Susan got a good education. The Quakers, or Friends as they

were known, had a rare respect for women and saw them equal to men intellectually and morally. Quaker women could speak (testify) during religious services and even serve as ministers. Also, while most of society thought it a sad fate to remain single, Quakers considered "spinsterhood" a downright respectable choice.

At her mother's knee, Susan learned that idleness is the root of all evil. Every day, she rose before daybreak, helped dress and feed the younger children, then attended school. After school came mountains of housework, including baking two dozen loaves of bread for the household.

When Susan was about 11, she began to fill in at the mill when workers were sick or absent. Later Susan said this experience opened her eyes about sex discrimination. In the mill, women earned half as much as men for doing the same kinds of jobs and never got promoted. This didn't seem right to Susan, so she suggested to her father that one of the workers, a smart and talented woman, be promoted to foreman. To Susan's dismay, her father said that was impossible, for it would be highly improper for a woman to supervise male workers.

As a teenager, Susan attended a Quaker boarding school in Philadelphia, where she earned a reputation for being smart but willful. Even though Quakers valued education for girls, they only let it go so far. Susan was a math whiz but got little encouragement. One day she got up the nerve to stand up and ask for division problems to solve. "Sit down, Miss Anthony," her teacher scolded. "Girls don't need division." Susan never forgot that, and when she began teaching at a Quaker school in upstate New York, her female students did plenty of math.

Because she was female, Susan earned $2.50 a week. Meanwhile, the male teachers earned $10 weekly. Feeling this wasn't at all fair, Susan marched to the board of education to tell them so: "Don't you think it's wrong to use women as cheap labor?" The board responded by firing Susan!

Luckily, girls' schools were cropping up all over and desperately needed teachers. Susan quickly found another job, where for the first time she was surrounded by non-Quakers. Being exposed to new ideas

THE MILL GIRLS

In preindustrial America, most women and girls spun their own wool and wove their own cloth. (Wealthy women hired weavers to do it for them and imported finer fabric from Europe.) But in the early 1800s, new technologies gave rise to mechanized mills (water- or steam-powered) with spinning machines and power looms. All over the Northeast, farms were mechanizing, too, so fewer young farm children were needed at home. Instead, the daughters got jobs in the new mills, while the sons found work in new shoe factories, telegraph offices, and print shops.

MILL GIRLS WORKED LONG HOURS AND SENT THEIR EARNINGS HOME TO THEIR FAMILIES.

Some of the mills were midsized, like the one managed by Susan's father. Others were huge. In Lowell, Massachusetts, tens of thousands of young girls and women left home to work in a mile-long spread of industrial five-story mills. The women lived in company-owned boarding houses and published their own newspaper, the *Lowell Offering*. At first, life in the cotton mill town was pretty good, but working conditions declined over time. In response, the women organized unions and pushed for shorter workdays (8 hours instead of 10 or 12) and a safer environment. In Lowell and similar mill towns, the factory way of life gave birth to the beginnings of a labor movement that would rock the nation a few decades later. Some factory girls wrote this poem about mill conditions:

LOWELL, MASSACHUSETTS, FACTORY GIRLS PUBLISHED THEIR OWN MAGAZINE, WHICH CALLED FOR BETTER WORKING CONDITIONS.

> Amidst the clashing noise and din
> Of the ever beating loom
> Stood a fair young girl with throbbing brow
> Working her way to the tomb.

and customs made her get just a little wild. She traded her plain Quaker dresses for soft pastels and modest frills and took romantic carriage rides with eligible bachelors. When the young men started to get serious, however, Susan politely nipped romance in the bud. "I don't want to be a drudge or a doll," she had decided. "Independence is happiness."

While teaching, Susan joined a temperance group, and it annoyed her that it was taboo for women to speak at meetings. "They say women should stick to their spheres," she said. "It would be ridiculous to speak of male and female atmospheres, male and female springs or rains, male and female sunshine. How much more ridiculous it is to talk of male and female spheres."

In the late 1840s, Susan inherited some money that allowed her to give up teaching and take up a life of activism. Like many other onetime temperance advocates, Susan switched her attention to the antislavery campaign, then to the women's rights crusade. First, she worked for the American Anti-Slavery Society in New York; then after the Seneca Falls women's rights convention of 1848, she spoke out just as often for women's rights. At Seneca Falls, Susan first met the reformer Elizabeth Cady Stanton, and the two soon formed a powerful working partnership. "I forged the thunderbolts," Elizabeth said. "And Susan fired them."

In the late 1850s, Susan tirelessly stumped (the term comes from speakers climbing onto tree stumps to address crowds!) all over New York, lobbying for a state Married Women's Law. It passed, which was a major victory for women. For the first time, married women in New York could own property, be the guardians of their own children, and file lawsuits. By 1860, fourteen states had passed similar laws.

Just as the women's rights movement was gaining steam, however, the Civil War erupted. The movement faded into the background until the war ended; then it sputtered to life again, quickly splitting into two camps. Voting rights for blacks (black men, that is) was the hot issue after emancipation, and Susan and her allies fully supported that; yet they also demanded the vote for black and white women. Another camp

☆≡☆≡☆≡☆≡☆≡☆≡☆≡☆≡☆≡☆≡☆≡☆≡☆≡☆≡☆≡☆≡

ELIZABETH CADY STANTON

Elizabeth Cady Stanton always remembered the moment she first met the somber Susan B. Anthony in 1848. "There she stood," Elizabeth wrote, "with her good earnest face and genial smile, dressed in a gray dress and hat, the perfection of neatness and sobriety. I liked her thoroughly."

The women worked together on women's rights issues from that day forward. Often they had heated arguments, but it was just their way of keeping each other on their toes. "It is better to be a thorn in the side of your friend than just her echo," Elizabeth said. "If this adds weight and stability to friendship, then ours will endure forever."

It did last forever, too. For half a century, Elizabeth mostly worked from home, where she was raising several children. She wrote articles, petitions, and speeches. Susan joined her in that task when taking breathers from the lecture circuit. Elizabeth's husband, Henry, said: "Elizabeth stirs up Susan, and Susan stirs the world."

☆≡☆≡☆≡☆≡☆≡☆≡☆≡☆≡☆≡☆≡☆≡☆≡☆≡☆≡☆≡☆≡

heartily disagreed with that approach, though. This group argued: "It is the Negro man's hour. Women need to wait a little longer." As you can imagine, Susan didn't agree. "Women have taken a back seat for too long," she explained. "We must join forces and win suffrage for all."

In 1868 and 1870, Susan and her allies lost the fight to change the language of the Fourteenth and Fifteenth Amendments to the Constitution so that both white and black women could vote. After that, Susan would never again fight for any cause but women's suffrage. Even her religious views were tied up in this cause. "I pray every single second of my life, not on my knees, but with my work," she said. "And my prayer is to lift women to equality with men."

To rally support for her cause, Susan founded a newspaper called *The Revolution.* The masthead read: "Men their rights and nothing more;

☆≡☆≡☆≡☆≡☆≡☆≡☆≡☆≡☆≡☆≡☆≡☆≡☆≡☆≡☆≡☆≡

THE FOURTEENTH AND FIFTEENTH CONSTITUTIONAL AMENDMENTS

The Fourteenth Amendment of the Constitution, adopted in 1868, guaranteed black men the same rights as white men. It forbade any state to deny the right to vote to "any of the male inhabitants" 21 or older. It was the first time that the word *male* had ever been written into the Constitution, instead of *people* or *citizens.* This distressed the women's suffrage camp greatly.

The Fifteenth Amendment also dealt with voting rights and was passed because some states had been keeping blacks from voting. The amendment proclaimed that the federal government and state governments could not "deny the right to vote based on race, color, or previous condition of slavery."

women their rights and nothing less." Susan also served as the long-time president of the National Woman Suffrage Association (NWSA), which had chapters in most major cities and many small towns. In her trademark red shawl, Susan visited group after group, rallying the troops.

On November 5, 1872, Susan decided to take a dramatic step to focus the nation's eyes on women's suffrage. With fourteen other women, she broke the law—on purpose. Susan and her partners in crime walked into a polling place in Rochester, New York. Then, before anyone could stop them, the women grabbed pencils to vote for Ulysses S. Grant for president. For breaking the law, Susan expected to be, and was, arrested. That, of course, fit right into her plan—for there is no better way to get attention than a trial.

In January 1873, Susan's case went to trial before a packed courtroom. The district attorney charged Susan with the crime of voting, saying: "At that time she was a woman, and the law does not say women can vote."

To that Susan's amused lawyer responded: "Your honor, gentlemen of the jury, the defense concedes that Miss Susan B. Anthony is indeed a woman—and that is why she is on trial. If her brother had voted, it would have been honorable. But because she is a woman, it is a crime. I believe this is the first instance in which a woman has been tried in criminal court simply because she is a woman."

Later in the trial, Susan was about to take the stand in her own defense, when the judge made a surprise move. He pronounced her "incompetent to testify," then ended the trial by *ordering* the jury to find her guilty. Many Americans who had followed the trial through newspaper accounts felt that Susan had been treated unfairly. The judge's highhandedness backfired, and support for Susan and her cause grew.

The judge, probably smarting from the criticism, let Susan speak at her sentencing. He probably wished he hadn't, though, for she declared: "I have many things to say. In your ordered verdict of guilty, you have trampled underfoot every vital principle of our government. My natural rights, my civil rights, my political rights, my judicial rights are all alike ignored."

At that, the judge nearly burst a blood vessel. "The court orders the prisoner to sit down," he shouted. "You are ordered to pay $100 in fines or go to jail." Susan shot back: "I shall never pay a dollar of your unjust penalty. Resistance to tyranny is obedience to God."

Susan was angry all right, but she also defied the judge because she *wanted* to be thrown in jail (so that even more people would support her and the cause). Susan also wanted to take the case to a higher court, in hopes that it would reinterpret the Constitution to define *citizen* as both male and female. That legal tactic was denied Susan, however, for after the judge calmed down, he wised up. Susan B. Anthony never paid her fine, but, to her disappointment, no police ever arrived to arrest her.

Free in spite of her best efforts, Susan shifted her attention to getting Congress to pass a new constitutional amendment giving women the vote. For forty long years, Congress repeatedly voted down what later came to be called the Susan B. Anthony Amendment. Still, right up to her death in 1906, Susan never gave up the fight.

In the 1880s, with her friend Elizabeth Stanton, Susan wrote *History*

THIS 1896 CAR-
TOON POKES FUN
AT ANTHONY
AND STANTON BY
SHOWING THEM
AS HEAVENLY
FIGURES ALONG-
SIDE GEORGE
WASHINGTON.

of Woman Suffrage. In the 1890s, she helped organize an International Council of Women. At the end of the century, pushing 80, she told friends she intended to die in the saddle, and that she did. In 1906, two days before dying of pneumonia at age 86, Susan gave her final speech at an annual NWSA convention. "I am here for a little time only," she said, "and then my place will be filled. The fight must not cease. You must see that it does not stop. Failure is impossible."

After Susan's death, "Failure is impossible" became the rallying cry of a new generation of suffrage leaders, who eventually won their prize. It took a very long time, but a hundred years after Susan B. Anthony's birth, Congress passed the Nineteenth Amendment to the Constitution. On November 2, 1920, 8 million American women voted for the very first time.

WOMEN AND VOTING IN THE WEST

Long before the federal Constitution granted women the right to vote, individual states did. From the 1860s through the 1890s, women got the vote in Wyoming Territory, Utah Territory, Colorado, and Idaho. Activists like Esther Morris of Wyoming and Abigail Duniway of Oregon lobbied for women's suffrage for the same reasons as Susan B. Anthony. And some male leaders supported women voting because it suited the needs of western states and territories with small populations. Having more voters meant that the West could wield more power nationally.

Sojourner Truth

(1 7 9 7 – 1 8 8 3)

I n 1864, two of the most beloved people in the United States met in the White House: President Abraham Lincoln and Sojourner Truth. After being shown into his office, Sojourner thanked the president for freeing the slaves. Then she mentioned she'd never heard of him before he became president. In response, Abe Lincoln smiled and said: "Ah, but I had heard of you many times before that."

SOJOURNER TRUTH MEETING WITH PRESIDENT ABRAHAM LINCOLN.

The striking woman who stood before Abraham Lincoln was born a slave in 1797. The second youngest of a dozen children born to James and Elizabeth Baumfree, Isabella (as Sojourner was originally called) grew up on several upstate New York farms owned by Dutch-speaking families. In Dutch the name *Baumfree* means "tall and straight tree." Isabella's father was given the name because he was tall and strapping, as was Isabella as a grown woman.

Isabella spent her earliest years in a snug little cabin that had a plot of land beside it for growing tobacco and corn. On Sunday, the slaves' day of rest, the Baumfree family sold crops they grew at market, and with the money bought food and clothing. That "good life" didn't last long, however, for the family's next owner housed them in a dark, damp basement with dozens of other slaves. There Isabella had only her parents and a younger brother, Peter, for the older siblings had all been sold.

One terrible day, Isabella herself felt the pain of separation, when a white man grabbed the screaming Peter, thrust him into a cage, and drove away with him. The memory of his crying was burned into her memory, as was the memory of that night. Isabella found her mother sitting alone in the dark, gazing into a star-filled night sky. "God lives in the sky and hears and sees you, child," her mother said. "He sees your brothers and sisters, too, and will look after them."

When Isabella was about 9, her mother and father were quite old. Their master freed them, and a friendly white family with no slaves gave them a cabin to live in and a plot of ground for gardening. Isabella wasn't so lucky. She was sold at auction to a storekeeper, John Nealy of Kingston, New York, along with a lot of sheep. After that, Isabella only saw her parents on rare visits, and she was beaten often for not understanding or speaking English. Up until then, Isabella's only language was Dutch, the language of her previous owners.

After a couple of years with the storekeeper, Isabella was relieved to be sold to a tavern keeper and fisherman, Mr. Scriver. There she enjoyed a "wild, out-of-door kind of life" carrying fish, hoeing corn, and digging roots for beer making. She was never beaten and liked the work, with one exception. Isabella had been taught by her mother never to use bad language, and she hated Scriver's fondness for "swearing and cussing." Isabella also inherited from her mother a deep faith, which pulled her through impossibly hard times.

When Isabella was about 13, she was sold again, and for the last time. At the farm of John Dumont, Isabella blossomed into a slender yet muscular 6-foot-tall woman. Although she was treated well most of the time, John Dumont did whip her once for sneaking out to meet a slave boy she liked. Like most slave owners, Dumont did not let his slaves pick their own mates. Instead, when Isabella was about 18, Dumont married her to Thomas, one of his other slaves. (Another slave performed a simple ceremony, which was the custom in this area and time.) Although some arranged slave marriages turned into loving relationships, this wasn't true for Isabella and Thomas. Yet between 1815 and 1826, they are known to have had at least four children together: Diana, Peter, Elizabeth, and Sophia.

Isabella was in her late twenties when she gave birth to her last child, Sophia, in about 1826. Life seemed to be looking up, for in 1827 a New York law would free slaves who had been born before 1799. John Dumont, however, had promised to free Isabella earlier, and let her take Sophia with her. (The law did not free Isabella's other children, who were born after 1799, so they had to stay with their master.) When Dumont broke his promise, Isabella was crushed. "I was foolish enough to keep feeding myself with that promise," she later recalled. "And when it was broken, I couldn't bear it."

Isabella was more than crushed, though—she was fed up. Unable to stand slavery for another moment, she got up one day before dawn. Then, with baby Sophia in her arms, she set out for freedom. Isabella headed for the farm of a local Quaker, Mr. Van Wagoner, who opposed slavery. As she'd hoped, he provided refuge—and something more. He protected Isabella and Sophia from their owner, John Dumont, when he stormed in demanding his slaves' return. First Van Wagoner tried to convince Dumont that slavery was a sin. When that failed, to protect Isabella and Sophia, Van Wagoner bought them.

Legally, this meant that Mr. Van Wagoner then owned Isabella (and her daughter), but the farmer despised slavery. So when Isabella called him master, he set the record straight. "You only have one master, as do I," he said. "And that is God." Van Wagoner paid Isabella wages for farm and housework, the first she'd ever earned.

On July 4, 1827, Isabella still lived at the Van Wagoner farm when the New York law came into effect freeing her—and 10,000 other New York slaves. Worry followed on the heels of joy, however, for Isabella learned that John Dumont had sold her 11-year-old son, Peter, to a slaveholder in Alabama. (Peter had not been freed by New York state law, for he was born after 1799, but Dumont had broken another state law that forbade the sale of slaves out of state.) With Van Wagoner's help, Isabella went to court and got Peter returned. The sympathetic judge also freed Peter, and Isabella was overjoyed. "For the first time, I felt tall within," she said. "I felt as if the power of a nation was with me, for my son had no other master, no other controller, no other conductor, but his mother."

One day soon after this victory, Isabella went for a walk in the woods. She sat under a willow tree by a stream, said a prayer, and had a vision in which God said: "There is no place on earth that I am not. Go forth and seek the truth." Inspired, Isabella joined the Methodist Church and moved to New York City in 1829.

Two decades of seeking the truth followed, in both New York and Massachusetts. Isabella worked as a housekeeper for idealists, reformers, and religious leaders, and for a time Sophia and Peter were with her. However, when Sophia was quite young, she either died or went back to live with her father (the record is unclear). And as a teenager, Peter left on a whaling ship and was never heard from again.

During these years, Isabella's spiritual quest led her to explore different denominations and beliefs. She regularly attended two Methodist churches: one with a black congregation and one with a white congregation. She also visited Quaker and Unitarian services, as well as tent revivals where people fell into trances and spoke in tongues. Isabella preferred quiet services to more emotional ones because she couldn't "hear God through all that noise and tumult."

For a time Isabella worked for and followed a self-declared prophet, Robert Matthews; then she joined a group that believed the world would end in 1843. Isabella also lived in a Northampton, Massachusetts, community of reformers trying to escape from a society they considered unjust and corrupt. In about 1843, the abolitionist leaders William Lloyd Garrison and Frederick Douglass visited an encouraged Isabella to speak publicly about her life and religious beliefs.

The Northampton community broke up in 1846, but Isabella made Florence, Massachusetts, her home base for several years. Most of the time, however, she was traveling about the North, speaking at churches, tent revivals, and abolitionist rallies. Standing before hundreds, Isabella

ANNA MURRAY DOUGLASS

You've probably heard of Frederick Douglass, the leading abolitionist who wrote three autobiographies detailing his life as a slave, a fugitive, and a reformer. But do you know about his remarkable wife, Anna Murray Douglass? This unsung heroine, born in 1813, married Frederick in 1838. Anna held weekly antislavery meetings for women, helped organize antislavery fairs, raised five children (mostly in the Rochester, New York, area), and harbored many fugitive slaves in her home. While doing all this, Anna also paid most of the household bills working as a shoe binder and laundress.

introduced herself using a new name she'd chosen: Sojourner Truth. It meant, she explained, searcher of the truth.

"Children, I talk to God, and God talks to me," Sojourner announced in a firm and motherly tone. Then she unleashed a hypnotic sermon that moved people to tears and laughter. She also had plenty of snappy comebacks for her critics. "Old woman, I don't care any more for your talk than I do for the bite of a flea," a man once shouted. "Perhaps not," Sojourner shot back, "but the Lord willing, I'll keep you scratching."

Because she had come through so much, seemed so strong, and was such a dynamic speaker, Sojourner fascinated both white and black audiences. Harriet Beecher Stowe (the author of *Uncle Tom's Cabin,* a novel that stirred abolitionist sentiment) said an inner light seemed to shine from Sojourner. Educated people asked her how she came to preach so well, despite not being able to read. Sojourner explained she'd memorized many passages of the Bible. She also said: "I can't read little things like letters, but I can read big things like men."

In 1850, Sojourner was in demand as a speaker for the abolitionist cause after the publication of her dictated memoirs, *The Narrative of Sojourner Truth: A Northern Slave.* With the proceeds and donations from friends, she was able to buy a small house in upstate New York,

HARRIET BEECHER STOWE'S *UNCLE TOM'S CABIN*

Harriet Beecher Stowe of Ohio wrote a best-selling novel, *Uncle Tom's Cabin*, after seeing a runaway slave crossing a river with a baby in arms. Her 1851 antislavery novel sold 3 million copies and drew so much attention that when President Abraham Lincoln met Harriet in 1862, he said: "So you are the little woman who wrote the book that started this great war!"

Building on the success of her first book, Harriet also wrote a nonfiction book documenting the horrors of slavery, *A Key to Uncle Tom's Cabin*. And with the proceeds from her writing, she supported a school for black girls in Washington, D.C.

which became her home base. But more often than not, she was on the road, making audiences weep from her tales of starving children, separated families, and terrible punishments of slaves. More than once, Sojourner was run out of town by hostile mobs.

Despite the danger, Sojourner never hesitated to speak her truths—even when it meant challenging her fellow reformers. At a public meeting in Boston's Faneuil Hall, she and Frederick Douglass were set to address a packed house. Douglass spoke first and ended his speech by saying that blacks needed the right to bear arms to protect themselves. "It must come to blood; they must fight for themselves, and redeem themselves," he said. Sojourner, who decried violence and believed God would ensure justice, stood up next, faced Frederick Douglass, and challenged loudly: "Frederick, is God dead?"

Sojourner wasn't afraid of challenging anyone, in fact. Once a rumor spread that she was a man in disguise, and several matrons cornered Isabella to inspect her chest. She stood before them, ripped open her blouse, and said: "Here, see for yourself. Here are the breasts that were forced to nurse white children instead of my own."

Like other abolitionists, Sojourner soon was addressing women's rights issues. Her ideas shook things up, too, for she forced the mostly white reformers (and the entire country) to consider the status, condition, and rights of black women, as well as white ones. In 1851, at an Akron, Ohio, convention, she made her thoughts crystal clear in what became a famous speech (see sidebar on next page). A minister there was speaking against the vote for women, saying that the dainty dears would faint when exposed to the ballot. Sojourner rose and said, according to the conference recording secretary, Marius Robinson:

> I want to say a few words about this matter. I am a woman's rights. I have as much muscle as any man, and can do as much work as any man. I have plowed and reaped and husked and chopped and mowed, and can any man do more than that? I have heard much about the sexes being equal. I can carry as much as any man, and can eat as much too, if I can get it. I am as strong as any man that is now. As for intellect, all I can say is, if a woman has a pint, and a man a quart—why can't she have her little pint full? You need not be afraid to give us our rights for fear we will take too much—for we can't take more than our pint'll hold. The poor men seems to be all in confusion, and don't know what to do. Why children, if you have woman's rights, give it to her and you will feel better. . . . And how came Jesus into the world? Through God who created him and the woman who bore him. Man, where was your part? But the women are coming up blessed be God and a few of the men are coming up with them. But man is in a tight place, the poor slave is on him, woman is coming on him, he is surely between a hawk and a buzzard.

In 1856, Sojourner moved to Battle Creek, Michigan, where a daughter and two grandsons lived. During the Civil War, Sojourner advocated giving free land to blacks in the West and abolishing the death penalty. She also collected supplies for black Union soldiers, one of whom was her grandson, James Caldwell. He fought with the 54th Regiment, Massachusetts Volunteers (the unit portrayed in the movie *Glory,* about black Civil War soldiers).

After the war, Sojourner continued to preach and lecture, agreeing with Susan B. Anthony (see chapter 3) that men and women of both colors should get the vote: "There is a great stir to give colored men their rights, but not a word about the colored woman. If colored men get their rights, and colored women don't get theirs, colored men will be the masters over the women, and it will be just as bad as before."

By the time of her death in 1883, Sojourner Truth had convinced a new generation of women of their inborn strength. "If the first woman God ever made was strong enough to turn the world upside down all alone," Sojourner said, "women together ought to be able to turn it back and get it right side up again."

✮≋✮≋✮≋✮≋✮≋✮≋✮≋✮≋✮≋✮≋✮≋✮≋✮≋✮≋✮≋✮≋

SOJOURNER'S TRUE WORDS

Several different versions of Sojourner's Akron, Ohio, speech exist. The version of conference recording secretary Marius Robinson recorded in this chapter was written down soon after Sojourner spoke, so many historians consider it the most authentic. However, Sojourner didn't like having her speeches quoted with any dialect (she thought it made her sound uneducated), so it might have been removed. The more colorful "Ain't I a Woman?" version of the speech is more famous and recognized, although it wasn't written down until twelve years after Sojourner spoke. Here's part of that version:

That man over there says that women need to be helped into carriages, and lifted over ditches, and to have the best place everywhere. Nobody ever helps me into carriages, or over mud-puddles, or gives me any best place! And ain't I a woman? Look at me! Look at my arm! I have ploughed and planted, and gathered into barns, and no man could head me! And ain't I a woman? I could work as much and eat as much as a man—when I could get it —and bear the lash as well! And ain't I a woman? I have borne children, and seen most all sold off to slavery, and when I cried out with my mother's grief, none but Jesus heard me! And ain't I a woman?

≋✮≋✮≋✮≋✮≋✮≋✮≋✮≋✮≋✮≋✮≋✮≋✮≋✮≋✮≋✮≋✮

Part Two

✦≈✦≈✦≈✦≈✦≈✦≈✦≈✦≈✦

SAVIORS AND LEADERS

★≋★≋★≋★≋★≋★≋★≋★

Clara Barton

(1 8 2 1 – 1 9 1 2)

A s a child, Clara Barton was as skittish as a rabbit. When thunderstorms hit, she burrowed under the covers and stuck her fingers in her ears. When bulls were slaughtered on her farm, she shivered with dismay. To her, the world was a dangerous place where she never felt quite safe. Yet as Clara grew older, she mustered the determination to conquer every fear. One day that determination would send her all the way to the front lines of the Civil War.

Clara was born on Christmas Day, 1821, into a well-off farm family in North Oxford, Massachusetts. Her parents, Stephen and Sarah Barton, had abolitionist sentiments, strongly believed in education for both boys and girls, and loved their five children. Clara often nestled in her father's lap as he told of being a soldier on the frontier, fighting against the warrior chief Tecumseh. (Later her knowledge of military life would serve her well.) Clara also admired her strong-willed mother and much older siblings, two boys and two girls. Yet despite these family strengths, she was often unhappy as a child, mostly because her parents argued loudly and often. When they did, Clara covered her ears and ran to hide, not emerging until the storm was over.

Clara found a port in the storm at school. On her very first day there,

★≋★≋★≋★≋★≋★≋★≋★≋★≋★≋★≋★≋★≋★

the teacher discovered that Clara was far ahead of children her own age. The teacher put "the little scholar" in a higher grade. Surrounded by older children, Clara felt shier than ever, but at least she wasn't bored. She was always curious, always reading, always learning new things. Once Clara asked a paperhanger to teach her to hang wallpaper and a carpenter to teach her to hammer a nail. She also got her brothers to teach her to throw a ball, tie sailor's knots, and saw boards. She even had enough courage to ride a horse bareback. There was no end to Clara's hunger to learn.

When Clara was 11, she did her first nursing. After her brother, David, fell from a barn roof and hurt himself badly, she took care of him for nearly two years. When the doctor said he'd never recover, Clara refused to believe it. She stayed by his side until he was well, which David said happened because Clara had a special "healing touch."

Nursing made Clara feel useful and needed, so when neighbors began to ask her to nurse their sick, she did. She even nursed victims of the highly contagious smallpox, despite the risk of getting it herself. "Perfect love," she said, "casts out fear." As a devout member of the Universalist Church, Clara believed in loving and serving others.

When Clara became a teenager, she began to fret about what her future would hold. Marriage, she later explained, frightened her, and the alternative was to work. Nursing wasn't an option because everyone considered it a charitable duty, not a profession. The textile mills wouldn't hire her, either, for at 5 feet tall she couldn't reach the looms, and the idea of teaching made Clara's stomach churn with anxiety.

Then, when Clara was about 16, an eccentric man named Lorenzo Fowler came to visit her church. By "mapping" bumps on heads, Fowler said he could discover people's true characters. Fowler called this "new science" phrenology. Clara had her head "read," and Fowler gave his verdict: "She is shy and sensitive. She won't ever assert herself—for herself—but for others she will be fearless. She should be a teacher."

Fowler's declaration gave Clara the confidence to find a teaching job. Although nervous at first, she was also clever. When the four biggest boys in class began to bully Clara, she took them out to play ball. That settled the bullies right down, for Clara had a wicked pitch that won their respect. After that, peace reigned in the classroom.

Until her early thirties, Clara taught in Massachusetts and New Jersey. She also reformed the educational system wherever she went, which earned her much respect. Clara convinced school boards to fix up ramshackle buildings, build new schools, and buy new books. In Bordentown, New Jersey, Clara even convinced officials to open the first public school in the state. Two years later, it had 600 students.

Although proud of her accomplishments, Clara grew less satisfied with her life. The more she taught, the more she longed for a better edu-

PHRENOLOGY

Phrenology was a fad of the late 1830s and 1840s. Some women even changed hairstyles to show off their cool bumps. In New York City, Lorenzo Fowler's Phrenological Cabinet displayed charts of famous heads. The poet Edgar Allen Poe, the author and humorist Mark Twain, and the Mormon leader Brigham Young were among them.

According to Fowler, each bump was linked to a particular part of the body. The size and shape of it showed a person's character and state of health. (The bumps could be made bigger or smaller with special exercises.) Of course, Fowler's success really stemmed from having insights into people's personalities.

Not everyone fell for the fad. Mark Twain, who wrote *Huckleberry Finn*, *Tom Sawyer*, and a lot of humorous pieces, said this about his first experience of having Fowler read his head: "He found a cavity, in one place; a cavity where a bump would have been in anyone else's skull. That cavity, he said, represented the total absence of a sense of humor."

Then Twain said this about his second visit to Fowler (after Fowler had found out Twain's true identity): "Once more he made a striking discovery. The cavity was gone and in its place was a Mount Everest—figuratively speaking—31,000 feet high, the loftiest bump of humor he had ever encountered in his life-long experience!"

cation herself. In 1850, when she was 29, Clara realized her dream and went back to school. At the Clinton Liberal Institute for Higher Learning, in Clinton, New York, Clara was a top student. She took very difficult classes, too, including analytic geometry, calculus, astronomy, German, French, ancient history, religion, and philosophy.

To Clara, college was heaven on earth, so it was a disappointing blow when family illness forced her to leave after only a year. Clara's mother died, then her father fell gravely ill. Clara had to support the family, so instead of returning to college, she found a good job as a school principal (thanks to her sterling reputation). When the job was taken from her and given to a man because it was more "fitting," Clara was so discouraged that she quit teaching

Needing a change, Clara packed her bags, headed for Washington, D.C., and in 1851 became a "government girl." The U.S. Patent Office in Washington, D.C., had just begun hiring women clerks. Clara liked the work and did it for several years. Discrimination followed her, though, and she didn't get deserved promotions. Even worse, some male coworkers treated the government girls like dirt. They blew smoke in Clara's face and spat tobacco on her shoes. When her supportive boss resigned in 1858, Clara did, too.

The Civil War ushered a new phase into Clara's life. Like so many Americans, Clara had read about a fearless European woman, Florence Nightingale, who had nursed the wounded during the Crimean War. Inspired by Florence Nightingale's example, Clara decided to act. Even thought her heart raced with nervousness, she ventured to the front lines to nurse the wounded.

On April 19, 1861, the first wounded of the Northern forces straggled into Washington after being attacked by a group of Southern sympathizers. Clara hurried to the Senate Chamber of the U.S. Capitol, where the wounded soldiers from the 6th Massachusetts Regiment had taken refuge. She treated what wounds she could, located lost luggage, wrote to soldiers' families, dished out soup, and organized other volunteers.

Then she set about rounding up desperately needed supplies, medicines, and food. Clara did the same in another makeshift hospital in Washington, D.C., after wounded arrived from the July 1861 Battle of Manassas in Virginia.

Clara worked miracles—everyone said so. Yet she felt as if she were putting a tiny bandage on a gaping wound. Supplies, medicines, and doctors were in short supply. Amputated limbs lay discarded in heaps, and bandages were dirty. The polluted drinking and bathing water resulted in outbreaks of typhoid, dysentery, and other diseases. It broke Clara's heart that many wounded soldiers would have escaped death if they'd been treated sooner and better.

Clara saw clearly what needed to be done. From every one of her

FLORENCE NIGHTINGALE

A small number of Catholic nuns and civilian women worked for the military as nurses during the American Revolution and the War of 1812. But female nursing as a profession didn't exist until Florence Nightingale came along. Born in 1820 in Italy and raised in England, Florence formed a nursing corps in 1853, during the Crimean War. The three-year European war was fought between Russia and a coalition that included England, France, and the Ottoman Empire (now Turkey). Florence recruited, trained, and supervised a group of volunteer female nurses—the first in world history. Thanks to her efforts, nursing emerged as a respected medical profession in Europe. Florence also wrote three books on nursing, which were translated into many languages, including English. In 1869, she founded the world's first nursing school in London.

CLARA WAS INSPIRED BY FLORENCE NIGHTINGALE, WHO IN THE 1850S ORGANIZED THE FIRST VOLUNTEER WOMEN'S NURSING CORPS IN EUROPE.

friends, former students, and family members, Clara begged for donations of supplies, medicines, and food. She ran newspaper advertisements requesting donations. The goods poured in so rapidly that Clara soon had to rent warehouses to hold everything.

Although Clara could have joined the new nursing corps being established by the federal government (see chapter 6), she preferred working alone. Plus she wanted to be right on the front lines, where help was needed the most. To get to the battlefields, however, Clara needed permission, and the military wasn't keen on women being near the fighting. Everywhere Clara turned, she found stumbling blocks—but her quiet determination paid off. When lower-level officials denied her requests, Clara went higher up, then higher up still. Soon everyone in government knew that Clara Barton simply couldn't be put off.

Permission for Clara to travel to the front lines finally came through on August 3, 1862. She gathered a caravan of supplies, donned a dark blue dress, and climbed into the lead wagon. She flicked a whip over the team of mules and headed to care for those who'd been wounded in the Battle of Cedar Mountain, in Culpepper, Virginia. Although she didn't arrive until four days after the battle, the needs of the wounded were still so great that Clara worked two straight days and nights with little rest.

SALLY LOUISA TOMPKINS

Virginia's Sally Louisa Tompkins moved among wounded on the front lines— the Confederate ones. After the first Battle of Bull Run at Manassas, she swiftly turned her Richmond home into a hospital; then she pestered leading citizens into providing her with needed supplies and funds. Confederate soldiers loved Sally (they called her "the lady with the milk-white hands"), and Jefferson Davis so admired her that he commissioned her an honorary captain of cavalry. After the war, Sally spent her entire fortune helping needy veterans, then joined the poor at Richmond's Home for Confederate Women. After her death in 1916, Sally was buried with full military honors.

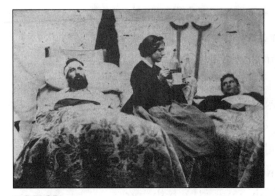

For the next few years, Clara was on the front lines at most of the major Civil War battles, from the Second Battle of Bull Run, Harper's Ferry, and South Mountain to Petersburg, Antietam, Fredericksburg, and Richmond. Often she was the first nurse on the field after troops retreated. Planting a white flag of truce amidst a sea of dead, Clara knelt on muddy, bloodsoaked ground to bandage wounds and speak words of comfort. She worked round the clock, patching up men and helping them into wagons bound for field hospitals. Later she said it was always in her mind that each man was "somebody's darling."

During the battle of Antietam, in September 1862, Clara drove up with her wagons just as Dr. James Dunn used his very last bandage to bind a wound. Despite flying bullets, she helped wounded on the field and was nearly killed when a bullet shot through the sleeve of her dress—and into the cheek of the wounded soldier. With her pocket-knife, she dug out the bullet. "I thought that night if heaven ever sent out a holy angel, she must be one," the doctor later said. After that, many people referred to Clara as the "angel of the battlefield."

After Antietam, Clara spent most of her time traveling with the Union Army of the Potomac. She spent bitter cold winter nights in a tent beside her wagon. She ate hardtack (hard, thick crackers issued by the army) with her boys and fed the runaway slaves who followed the Union Army to freedom. She washed faces, iced hot heads, and stood beside deathbeds. Soldiers hailed her with tears and cheers. When people tried to tell her the work was too difficult for a woman, Clara just looked at them and said with quiet dignity: "The fighting, you know, is far worse for men."

When the end of the war was in sight, in March 1865, President Lincoln granted Clara permission to establish and run the Office of Correspondence with Friends of the Missing Men of the United States Army. For four years, Clara worked tirelessly to locate missing soldiers and identify those who had died. Clara worked just as hard on this task as she had nursing soldiers, and by August 1865, she'd identified and marked the graves of 13,000 soldiers who died in captivity in Anderson Prison in Georgia. Four years later, when the office was disbanded, she'd identified a total of roughly 22,000 dead or missing.

The war turned Clara into an advocate for women's rights (she embraced women's suffrage) and peace. On a whirlwind lecture tour with other Civil War figures—including the abolitionist Frederick Douglass and the noted authors Ralph Waldo Emerson and Mark Twain—Clara gave 200 speeches. "All the suffering I've seen has taught me that war is the worst way to solve conflicts," she told audiences.

While lecturing in Europe in 1870, Clara was visited by a representative of the International Red Cross, an organization dedicated to helping the victims of war and natural disasters. To check out this organization's work, Clara traveled to the front lines of the ongoing war between France and Prussia. For four months, Clara assisted refugees from the war, then she worked in a hospital in Baden, Germany. Clara was more than impressed by the Red Cross, which she said accomplished more quality relief work in several months than had been done during America's entire Civil War. Clara's own contributions were so great that the emperor of Germany, Kaiser Wilhelm, awarded her an Iron Cross of Merit in 1873.

When Clara came home from her trip, she hoped to establish an arm of the Red Cross in the United States. The idea of an international organization wasn't popular, however, for many leaders feared it would undermine the independence and sovereignty of the United States. That's why it took Clara until 1882 to achieve her goal. One way Clara got support was to expand the mission of the organization. Instead of just providing assistance related to warfare, Clara designed the American Red Cross to help during floods, famines, droughts, epidemics, hurricanes, and other natural or manmade disasters.

For twenty-three years, Clara served as president of the American Red Cross, which became one of America's (and the world's) most respected relief organizations. As president, she directed the many chapters established in cities and small towns across America. From time to time, she also continued to serve on the front lines. At age 70, she took needed supplies to Cuba. At age 79, she helped the victims of flooding in Galveston, Texas. Not until 1904, at age 83, did Clara retire. She moved to Echo, Maryland, and several years later, in 1912, she died at age 91.

THE RED CROSS

Today 12,000 staff members and 20 million volunteers work in Red Cross organizations in 176 countries. In the United States, there are 2,800 chapters. Along with helping the victims of war, the Red Cross delivers food, clothing, medical supplies, and comfort to millions.

It all began in 1859 because the Swiss businessman Henry Dunant got caught behind the battle lines during a short-lived war between the Austrians and the French. Dunant helped tend the wounded in a church-turned-hospital, and it left such an impression on him that when he got home to Geneva, Switzerland, he organized an international meeting called the Geneva Convention.

The first 1859 Geneva Convention (it has since been amended many times) drew twenty-four delegates from sixteen governments. The delegates hammered out an agreement, which said that hospitals would not be military targets and all wounded (civilian, friend, or enemy) would receive equal and adequate treatment. The convention also established the International Committee of the Red Cross and chose as its symbol a bold red cross on a bright white background (the colors of the Swiss flag). Relief workers in nations bound by the treaty would fly a flag, hang signs, and wear armbands with the symbol so that armies would know not to harm them.

The Geneva Convention agreement was signed by all of the represented nations except Great Britain, Sweden, and the United States. However, the United States did sign later, in 1882. After that, the American Red Cross was chartered as the U.S. humanitarian organization that would carry out the principles of the Geneva Convention and its International Committee of the Red Cross.

Dorothea Dix

(1 8 0 2 – 1 8 8 7)

Someone with an iron will was needed to ensure that the U.S. military provided good care for wounded and dying soldiers of the Civil War. Dorothea Dix took on the job and moved mountains. Thanks to her, thousands of nurses saved countless lives. Thanks to her, nursing became a respected profession that was open to women.

Dorothea was born in Hamden, Massachusetts (later part of Maine), in 1802, but when she was very young her family moved to Worcester. Dorothea's family life was hard, for her father, Joseph, earned very little as a Methodist minister, and her mother, Mary, suffered from terrible headaches and other illnesses. When Dorothea's two younger brothers were born, it fell to her to care for them and to do all the housework. It was difficult work for a child (especially with no electricity or running water!), and Dorothea later recalled that she "never knew childhood."

Dorothea was raised to "do her duty," and she knew her family needed her, but she deeply longed to go to school. When she was about 12, that dream finally came true, for her wealthy Boston grandmother, Madame Dix, sent for her and her younger brothers to come and stay. Madame Dix could afford to send Dorothea to secondary school (public elementary schools were free, but private high schools for girls charged tuition), and Dorothea attended for two years. During that time, she hit the books hard and packed in a lot of learning.

Another kind of learning (which Dorothea wasn't as thrilled about) included lessons on how to become a "lady." All of a sudden, the little girl who'd had one tattered dress had dozens—plus a dance instructor! Such luxury was hard for Dorothea to adjust to, especially when beggar children gathered at the mansion's front gate. When 14-year-old Dorothea tried to give the beggar children some of her new clothes, her grandmother threw up her hands in despair and sent Dorothea off to a great-aunt in Worcester.

At her aunt's, Dorothea was happier than before, partly because she became good friends with an older cousin, Edward Bangs. Edward recognized Dorothea's intelligence and encouraged her to start a private school for girls. When she was only 15, in 1816, Dorothea did just that, and the school was quite successful. For three years, Dorothea taught twenty girls between ages 6 and 8.

For nearly twenty years, Dorothea ran her school, wrote five children's schoolbooks, and did charity work in the community. Then, when she was 39, a stint teaching Sunday school at a Boston women's prison inspired Dorothea with a burning mission. She had seen prisoners with mental problems jailed with criminals. Even more dreadful, the mentally ill were caged, beaten, and terribly neglected. Horrified and outraged, Dorothea left the jail, abandoned teaching, and used an inheritance from her grandmother to launch a one-woman campaign to reform the mental health system.

When it came to planning and organizing, Dorothea was a whiz. Her secret weapon was never jumping into things unprepared. To tackle the mental health issue, Dorothea traveled through Massachusetts for eighteen months visiting jails. With clipboard in hand, she wrote down everything she saw and heard. Only after a detailed report was printed and bound did she petition the state legislature to act.

Dorothea's petition to the Massachusetts state legislature read, in part:

I call your attention to the present state of Insane Persons confined within this Commonwealth, in cages, closets, cellars, stalls, and pens; chained, naked, beaten with rods, and lashed into obedience. I challenge you in the name of Christianity and humanity to put away the cold, calculating spirit of selfishness and self-seeking; lay off the armor of local strife and political opposition; raise up the fallen, succor the desolate, restore the outcast, defend the helpless.

At first, the offended legislators scolded Dorothea for sticking her nose where it didn't belong—in government business. Yet instead of despairing, Dorothea came up with a clever plan. She rallied support from leading male citizens, whom the legislators might take more seriously. Among these was Dr. Samuel Gridley Howe, the director of the New England Asylum for the Blind (and the husband of Julia Ward Howe, author of "The Battle Hymn of the Republic"). The support of Dr. Howe and others convinced the Massachusetts legislature to pass a law requiring humane treatment of the mentally ill.

With this first victory in hand, Dorothea was unstoppable. All over the nation, and even overseas, she investigated the treatment of the mentally ill. Dorothea bombarded state and federal officials with letters, reports, and petitions. Few could resist the full force of her conviction that publicly funded mental hospitals must be built. New Jersey legislators were the first to look up and find the unyielding Dorothea Dix planted before their desks, determined to be heard. One legislator said: "It would be cheaper to transport Dorothea Dix across the state line than establish an asylum!"

The lawmaker should have saved his breath, however, for in 1841, the New Jersey State Lunatic Asylum opened its doors in Trenton. Because the superintendent appreciated Dorothea's work on behalf of the mentally ill, he set aside an apartment for her to stay in when she wasn't off lobbying assorted officials and legislatures. (The result of those meetings was spectacular, too. When Dorothea began her campaign in 1841, 11 mental hospitals existed in America. When her campaign ended in 1860, there were 123.)

Dorothea was tired and needed a rest. But with the Civil War looming, she began to realize that the government wasn't at all prepared to meet the needs of American soldiers. Weaponry had become much more deadly since the Revolution and the War of 1812, and far more men would serve in the military. Dorothea wondered: Who would provide decent food, supplies, living conditions, and medical care—and how?

With these concerns in mind, Dorothea visited one of the nation's few female doctors, Dr. Elizabeth Blackwell, in New York City. Elizabeth had already founded the all-volunteer Women's Central Association of Relief for the Sick and Wounded of the Army, and Dorothea wanted to get together and discuss their common concerns. In early 1861, Dorothea also traveled to Washington, D.C., to witness the volunteer work being done by Clara Barton (see chapter 5).

Dorothea, Elizabeth, and a group of well-known reformers and doctors soon discovered that they shared the same concerns. In the past, soldiers recovering from their wounds were cared for by untrained recovering soldiers, military wives, and other volunteers. But this modern, large-scale war would require a new and comprehensive approach.

With Elizabeth and the other leading reformers, Dorothea discussed the need for a new agency with government powers. The proposed U.S. Sanitary Commission would oversee hospitals, collect and distribute supplies, and assist refugees and military families. It would also ensure sanitary conditions in military camps and provide expert nursing care by trained women.

No one ever called Dorothea Dix a bubbly or lovable person. Her mind was fixed on accomplishing whatever task she set for herself, and she didn't care if anyone liked her. Although some people thought Dr. Elizabeth Blackwell was the better candidate to run the nursing corps of the proposed commission, the doctor herself promoted Dorothea to the post. Male doctors would have a hard enough time accepting female nurses, Elizabeth said. It would be even more of a problem if they had to take directions from a female doctor.

In truth, Dorothea's nature and skills made her the perfect person to supervise nurses for the proposed U.S. Sanitary Commission. But getting government support was an uphill battle. One problem was that officials moved at a snail's pace, so again Dorothea tackled the government bureaucracy. She wrote a detailed report supporting the commission's establishment and proving why a corps of paid, trained women nurses was critical. Then she visited Secretary of War Simeon Cameron, presented the report, and passionately pleaded her case.

☆≡☆≡☆≡☆≡☆≡☆≡☆≡☆≡☆≡☆≡☆≡☆≡☆≡☆≡☆≡☆≡☆≡☆≡☆≡

DR. ELIZABETH BLACKWELL

In 1844, a young teacher who wanted to be a doctor threw herself into what she called a "great moral struggle." Elizabeth Blackwell applied to twenty-nine medical schools, including Harvard's and Yale's, only to be turned down flat. Undaunted, Elizabeth didn't give up, and eventually Geneva College accepted her. However, the college accepted her "by accident." Officials there thought the application was from a man! When Elizabeth showed up for classes, the entire college was in an uproar. Elizabeth was asked to leave, but she insisted on staying and did. Male students refused to work with her. Women in the town crossed the street when they saw her coming. When she sat down in the college dining room to eat, everyone ignored her. Still, Elizabeth was so smart and so determined that in 1849 she graduated at the *top* of her class, becoming America's first female licensed physician. Yet even with a degree in hand, Elizabeth's troubles weren't over, for hospitals in United States, England, and Europe banned her from treating patients. So in 1853, Elizabeth struck out on her own. She opened a clinic in a neighborhood of poor immigrants in New York City. During the Civil War, Elizabeth threw herself into establishing the U.S. Sanitary Commission, and after the war she founded a medical school for women.

☆≡☆≡☆≡☆≡☆≡☆≡☆≡☆≡☆≡☆≡☆≡☆≡☆≡☆≡☆≡☆≡☆≡☆≡☆≡

Dorothea told Secretary Cameron that too many men were cramped into tents, and raw sewage ran through camp, spreading disease. Dorothea also told the secretary that soldiers went without rations, and army doctors used outdated medicine and surgery. "The wounded men from the first skirmishes are only surviving by the grace of God and Clara Barton," she said. "More fighting is coming, and something must be done!"

Miffed by Dorothea's "sharp tongue," the secretary of war grumbled about "meddling women" and "pet causes." But after a few weeks, he gave in and the U.S. Sanitary Commission was established, with Dorothea Dix installed as superintendent of nurses.

At first, few officials thought the Sanitary Commission would really be important to the war effort. Even President Lincoln, when he signed the bill creating it, said: "Well, I can't see that it will be anything but a fifth wheel to the coach, but it is signed." In addition, most army surgeons weren't pleased, for they did not welcome the female nurses. A medical journal of the day stated that female nurses were "a useless annoyance" and lacked the physical strength to do the job. The article also suggested that its readers try to "imagine a delicate refined woman assisting a rough soldier with a bedpan."

Dorothea could imagine it all right, and she quickly set about hiring and training 4,000 nurses (from 40,000 applicants). The commission also opened offices in New York; Washington, D.C.; Boston; Philadelphia; Buffalo; Louisville; Chicago; and Detroit—and the organization worked closely with about 7,000 other local and regional aid societies.

Before long, it was plain as day to everyone that the commission and its nurses were heaven-sent. After just one 1862 battle, at Antietam, there were 23,110 casualties, and Dorothea's nurses were there, saving life after life. In addition, the commission passed out 29,000 shirts, 3,000 pounds of cereal, 2,600 pounds of condensed milk, 5,000 pounds of beef, 3,000 bottles of wine, 120 barrels of blankets, and 4,000 bed sheets.

As the first woman appointed to an executive position in the U.S. government, Dorothea was like a dog with a bone. She let nothing get

★彡★彡★彡★彡★彡★彡★彡★彡★彡★彡★彡★彡★彡★彡★彡

DR. MARY WALKER: CIVIL WAR SURGEON

In 1861, the U.S. Army had only 113 physicians, and 24 resigned to join the Confederacy. Four years later, 15,000 army surgeons had served in the Union and Confederate armies. Yet Dr. Mary Walker, who in 1855 became the second American woman to graduate from medical school, was the only female doctor to serve in the war.

Mary hounded Union officials until they finally hired her as an assistant surgeon in 1863. Then she shocked everyone by wearing pants! Her specially designed uniform was modeled after the bloomer costume that was popularized by Amelia Bloomer (see chapter 2). In Union circles, Mary wasn't popular, thanks to this act of rebellion, but she was tolerated because she saved lives. Confederates, however, freely heaped scorn on the woman doctor who dared to dress like a man: "Such a thing could be produced only by the debased and depraved Yankee nation," one disgusted rebel (Southern) officer scornfully told his wife.

After the war, Mary received a Congressional Medal of Honor, but it was taken away in 1917. Several people's medals were taken away because new rules said only those who'd seen combat should have gotten one (but Mary's family was convinced it was because she was female). In 1977, an army board reawarded the medal to Dr. Mary Walker, citing her "self-sacrifice, patriotism, dedication, and unflinching loyalty to her country, despite the apparent discrimination because of her sex."

★彡★彡★彡★彡★彡★彡★彡★彡★彡★彡★彡★彡★彡★彡★彡

in the way of the commission's success. For example, Dorothea only hired women who were smart, respectable, responsible, not too pretty, and over 30. If at all possible, Superintendent Dix didn't want attractive girls because she thought they might get involved in nurse-soldier romances. Middle-aged women, Dorothea also thought, would be less flighty and better able to get by on the pitiful wage (40 cents a day compared to $2 a day for the male inspectors, relief agents, clerks, and drivers). Dorothea wanted women who could put up with the dreadful army food, too. One nurse said the meat tasted as if it had been prepared by the men of 1776, and the stewed blackberries looked and tasted like stewed cockroaches!

Along with overseeing the nurses, Dorothea coordinated hospital inspections and the delivery of hospital supplies. Remarkably, for the first couple of years, she managed this without a dime of government money. Congress did not grant any funds for Sanitary Commission operations until two years into the war. Dorothea's efforts would surely have flopped if it hadn't been for an army of women in Soldiers and Ladies Aid Societies nationwide. The women organized massive "sanitary fairs" to raise money for the commission.

SOUTHERN NURSES

Roughly 2,000 women also worked as volunteer and paid nurses for the Confederacy. Southern society had a very hard time accepting women in such posts, but the Confederacy was in desperate need of health care providers. After the war, many of the Union nurses were able to establish careers as nurses or in related professions, but Southern women were expected to return to the home. The Confederate nurse Sarah Morgan of Louisiana bowed to society's wishes and desperately missed being useful. "If I was independent," she wrote in her diary, "if I could work on my own, I would not be poring over this stupid page, I would not be idly reading or sewing. I would put aside woman's trash and take up woman's duty. Yet it is impossible—chained bear, coward, helpless woman that I am. Oh, if I were free."

Dorothea worked without pay and slept on hospital floors. She was kind to hospital administrators (called matrons) if they worked hard and obeyed the rules. Being a complete stickler for rules and discipline won her some enemies among resentful hospital staff, but Dorothea didn't care. She knew that unsanitary conditions and slipshod care contributed greatly to soldiers' deaths from infections or diseases, such as typhoid, pneumonia, tuberculosis, and dysentery.

To catch the slackers, Dorothea prowled hospital corridors late at night, secretly checking up on the staff. No mistakes were tolerated, and no laziness went unreported. And what about those who dared dip into the barrel of whiskey kept to use as medicine? Watch out! "Dragon Dix is a self-sealing can of horror tied up in red tape," one grumbler said.

Among the hospital staff, Dorothea was most resented by male doctors who wanted to have the only authority over nurses. In October 1863, the government caved in to the doctors and took away Dorothea's responsibilities involving direct nursing supervision. Although she was fit to be tied, Dorothea swallowed her pride and continued what duties she had left.

After the war, Dorothea spent a year helping veterans get back on their feet and helping Southerners repair hospitals damaged during the war. Then, at age 63, she returned to helping the mentally ill. Dorothea Dix saved countless lives, improved life for the mentally ill, and established nursing as an honorable profession. Then in 1887, she died among friends, in the apartment set aside for her in a wing of a Trenton, New Jersey, mental institution—the very first hospital she'd helped establish.

CHAPTER 7

Harriet Tubman

(1820?-1913)

arriet Tubman braved vicious dogs and armed men to deliver hundreds of her people from slavery on the escape network called the Underground Railroad. When slaves heard the ex-slave's gravelly voice softly crooning familiar hymns, they knew Harriet was hiding nearby, ready to deliver them safely to the promised land.

The famous "railroad conductor" began life as Araminta Ross, a slave on a Bucktown, Maryland, plantation. Minty, as she was nicknamed, later came to be called Harriet, after her mother. Harriet and Benjamin Ross had between ten and thirteen children (no one's exactly sure because slave births weren't always recorded). Harriet's own birth date is also unknown, but was somewhere around 1820.

Harriet grew up in a one-room windowless shack in the slave quarters. She wore one sacklike dress and ate a lot of cornmeal mush. However, compared to many slave girls, Harriet had one stroke of good fortune. She lived with both of her parents and at least a few of her brothers and sisters. (The rest had been sent down river, which meant sold away from the family.)

While most plantation slaves were either field-workers or house slaves who did domestic work, Harriet's father had the job of cutting wood in the forest. When she was little, Harriet liked to go with her father to help. Harriet learned many things in the woods that would later come in handy, like how to read the stars to tell directions. She also learned how to safely cross rivers, imitate bird calls, gather wild foods, and trap small animals for meat.

When Harriet was about 6 years old, the master considered her old enough to send to the fields. Because Harriet was tiny for her age, her mother asked the master instead to hire Harriet out. (Slave owners often loaned their slaves to nonslaveholding neighbors for a fee.)

Although her mother meant well, Harriet's life wasn't any easier than it would have been in the fields. For the next couple of years, she worked for a weaver, a trapper, and a plantation mistress. At the weaver's, puffs of lint from the air filled her lungs and made her ill. Being sickly made her work slowly, so the weaver beat Harriet and then returned her to her master. Then Harriet was sent to work for a muskrat trapper and had to check traps in a cold river. That made her sick, too (and left her with a permanently gravelly voice). Finally, Harriet was sent to work as a nurse-maid, and the woman of the house ordered Harriet to never let the baby cry. Since babies cry when they are hungry, wet, tired, or for no reason at all, Harriet got punished there, too.

After all of these jobs didn't work out, the master sent 8-year-old Harriet to the fields after all. There she surprised everyone, for in the open air and sunshine, Harriet's health improved. In the bright bandana of a field-worker, Harriet soon grew tough as a nut. That didn't mean Harriet was content, though. Although she had no knowledge of freedom, she did have a growing sense of the injustice against her people.

When Harriet was about 12, she acted against that injustice. One day while working in the field, the plantation overseer (who bossed the slaves for the master) gave her a terrible order. A young field-worker standing near Harriet tried to run away. The overseer quickly cornered the man, then hollered to Harriet to hold him down. Harriet felt like a tree rooted to the ground. She couldn't do what the overseer ordered, for it was horrible and wrong. As Harriet stood there frozen in place, the overseer rushed by her toward the slave, and without thinking, Harriet threw herself between them. Red-faced and swearing, the overseer turned on Harriet and hit her with an iron weight. She tumbled to the ground, unconscious, her forehead bleeding from an 8-inch gash.

Although Harriet lost a lot of blood from the nasty wound, her mother nursed her back to health. Nothing, however, could rid Harriet of the large, dented scar on her forehead—or the terrible headaches she suffered for the rest of her life. Harriet's rebellion also earned her something far worse, for her angry master began talking about selling Harriet. Fate came to her aid, however, for the master died and his son inherited the slaves. Harriet later recalled, "I heard I was going to be sent like my brothers to the chain gang, and I prayed that if the Lord didn't change the master's heart, he would kill him and take him out of the way where he wouldn't do any more mischief!"

Instead of being sold, Harriet was sent to the woods to work with her father. Then at about age 24, Harriet married John Tubman, a free black man. (Marrying a free man did not change Harriet's slave status, and if she'd had any children, they would have been slaves, too.) John promised to help Harriet to buy her freedom or escape, but after they were married a while, he changed his tune. There was no sense spending money on freedom, he argued, when things were fine as they were. Plus, there was always a chance John would be caught helping Harriet escape, and the punishment was hanging.

For several years, Harriet tried to live with her disappointment and continued to work in the woods. But by 1849, the master's estate had been broken up, and she was to be sold to a slave trader. Harriet told John she was going to escape to the North with or without him. When he answered that he'd turn her in if she ran, Harriet decided he was bluffing and took off under the cover of night. "There was one of two things I had a right to," she said, "liberty or death; if I couldn't have one, I would have the other, for no man would take me alive."

Harriet left her husband, parents, and slavery behind—and ran like the wind. In the dead of night, she hurried to the home of a white family that she'd heard would help runaway slaves. The house was indeed a stop on the Underground Railroad, and the sympathetic owners welcomed Harriet. Tucked under some old sacks in the back of a produce wagon, Harriet was hustled to the next station and the next. Ninety miles later, after passing through Maryland, Delaware, and Pennsylvania, Harriet arrived in Philadelphia. As she set foot on free soil for the first time, Harriet looked at her hands to make sure she was the same person. "There was such a glory over everything," she said. "The sun came like gold through the trees and over the fields, and I felt like I was in heaven."

THE UNDERGROUND RAILROAD

Roughly 70,000 slaves traveled to freedom on the Underground Railroad, which ran from Maine to Nebraska, through fourteen states. It wasn't a real railroad, of course, but a series of secret escape routes and safe hiding places. "Freights" (runaway slaves) traveled along "lines" (routes) and stayed at "stations" (safe houses). "Station masters" gave slaves food, money, shelter, and encouragement. Legend has it that the escape network got its name when a slave owner couldn't find his runaway slave. "It's like he's vanished on some underground road," the slave owner grumbled.

Although a minority of runaway slaves stayed in the South (joining Native American tribes or creating free settlements in remote swamplands and mountains), most fled north on this Underground Railroad. In 1850, the new Fugitive Slave Act made escape to the Northern states more dangerous, so more went all the way to Canada. The law made it illegal to help escaped slaves, and in free states slaves could be caught and returned to their owners. Lawmen who knew about runaway slaves and did *not* arrest them could be fined $1,000 per slave.

In Philadelphia, Harriet found work as a domestic servant and made friends, but she missed her family and her people terribly. In her thoughts was a man she knew who had spent twenty-five years in prison. All the man thought of was when he would be free and able to see his family and friends again. But when the man was finally freed and went home, his house and family were gone and his name was forgotten. There was no one to welcome him. "So it was with me," Harriet explained. "I had crossed the line of which I had so long been dreaming. I was free. But there was no one to welcome me to the land of freedom. I was a stranger in a strange land." This feeling led Harriet to make a solemn resolution: "I was free, and my people should be free also. I would make a home for them in the North."

An organization called the Philadelphia Vigilance Committee, run by African Americans, helped slaves escape on the Railroad. Harriet heard of the group and went to see its leader, William Still. She offered her services as a guide for runaways, and after taking an oath of secrecy, she learned about safe house locations, station masters' identities, secret codes, and special signals. Harriet was taught how to use disguises for herself and the runaways. And she learned about planning escapes at just the right time so that runaways could stay one step ahead of the slave catchers and their bloodhounds.

Then Harriet went to work. For the next decade, on nineteen rescue missions, she guided more than 300 slaves to freedom. "I never ran my train off the track, and I never lost a passenger," Harriet said. Soon those grateful passengers gave her the nickname of Moses, after the Biblical prophet who led the slaves of Israel out of Egypt to freedom.

Harriet's first rescue was her own sister with her two children. Using special signals (so secret that many are still unknown), Harriet sent word to her sister back in Maryland to hide at night at a particular spot on the shores of the Chesapeake Bay. On the planned date, Harriet arrived in an old fishing boat and carried her sister and the children to freedom. Later, Harriet also rescued her mother, father, and other family members. In his diary, William Still wrote that he feared for Harriet's safety: "I was afraid for her, but she was without personal fear. The idea of being captured by slave-hunters or slaveholders, seemed never to enter her mind."

Harriet's first home base was St. Catherines, Ontario, in Canada—the end of the Underground Railroad line. (Many slaves went all the way to Canada to get beyond the reach of slave catchers, who tracked down some escaped slaves living in Northern states.) While in Canada, Harriet was introduced to the militant abolitionist John Brown. When he took her hand, he was so overwhelmed that he murmured: "General Tubman, General Tubman, General Tubman." From then on, that became another of Tubman's nicknames.

General Tubman was such a whiz as a conductor that plantation owners offered a $40,000 reward for her capture (that's like a million dollars in today's money). You might think that being barely 5 feet tall and having a big dented scar on her forehead would make Harriet easily recognized and caught, yet she outfoxed all who pursued her. Traveling at night, using the North Star as her compass, she crept down dirt paths and through dark forests to slave quarters or arranged meeting spots. Then in her throaty voice, Harriet quietly crooned spirituals. Slaves learned through the grapevine that certain hymns—"The Old Ark's a-Moven' Away," "You'd Better Run," "Git On Board," and "Go Down Moses"—meant the freedom train had arrived.

The runaways—from toddlers to gray-haired grandparents—trusted Harriet completely. Often dogs and armed men were at their heels, but Harriet was clever. She disguised light-skinned slaves as white masters, and women as men. She picked up slaves on Saturday night because runaway notices didn't appear in local newspapers until Monday. She used herb concoctions to quiet babies, and with her pistol Harriet threatened fearful slaves who wanted to turn back. "You'll die or be free," Harriet informed her passengers.

During the war, Harriet also ran a Union hospital for black refugees in Hilton Head, South Carolina. (For this work, Harriet was never paid.

ACCORDING TO ESTIMATES, MORE THAN 70,000 SLAVES TRAVELED TO FREEDOM ON THE UNDER-GROUND RAILROAD.

She supported herself by selling home-made bread and root beer!) Thousands of slaves followed the Union Army to freedom, and the bedraggled refugees came to the hospital, all skin and bones. Harriet nursed them back to health and helped find them jobs.

The Union Army also asked Harriet to do some spying. She posed as an ancient slave woman and went to the Confederate camps to gather information on troop movements and supplies. In 1863, a disguised Harriet ventured into swamps, jungles, and woodlands to locate several hundred slaves hiding there. With the information she brought back, the Union sent 150 black soldiers in the 2nd South Carolina Volunteers on a gunboat up the Combahee River to rescue the slaves.

When the gunboat stopped to collect about 800 slaves, Harriet watched alongside the captain. One woman brought on board a pot of steaming hot rice, as well as a black pig and a white pig. "We named the white pig Beauregard, and the black pig Jefferson Davis," Harriet said. (Jefferson Davis was the president of the Confederacy, and Pierre Beauregard was a Confederate field commander.)

When the war ended, Harriet relocated to Auburn, New York, where a friend, William Henry Seward (a former New York governor and U.S. senator who would soon be President Lincoln's secretary of state), loaned Harriet a two-story brick house (later he sold it to her). Harriet, whose husband, John, had died during the war, was widowed and had no income. So she asked the U.S. government for a pension for her wartime services.

The pension was denied, but in 1864 two developments helped ease her poverty. First, Harriet married a Union veteran, Nelson Davis. And, second, Sarah Hopkins Bradford wrote a book about Harriet's life and gave her the proceeds. *Scenes in the Life of Harriet Tubman* (later renamed *Harriet Tubman: The Moses of Her People*) also earned Harriet nationwide recognition. Offers to pay Harriet to lecture arrived, as did letters of support and admiration.

For the next two decades, Harriet spoke out often on the lecture circuit—for black rights, women's rights, and educational opportunities for blacks and women. After Nelson died in 1888, she also received a government pension at last, but for being a veteran's widow. Typically, Harriet didn't use the pension for herself but to help others. She founded the Harriet Tubman Home, which cared for old and poor ex-slaves (including, in her final years, herself).

In 1913, Harriet died peacefully in the Harriet Tubman Home, leaving a legacy of strength and determination. To honor that legacy, New York State celebrates March 10th as Harriet Tubman Day. A U.S. postage stamp also bears her likeness, and hundreds of schools and community centers all over America bear her name. Yet of all the tributes to Harriet Tubman, one may be the simplest and most true: "Harriet Tubman," said the women's rights crusader Susan B. Anthony, "was a most wonderful woman."

ABOLITIONIST FREDERICK DOUGLASS WROTE TO HARRIET IN 1868

The difference between us is very marked. Most that I have done and suffered in the service of our cause has been in public, and I have received much encouragement at every step of the way. You, on the other hand, have labored in a private way. I have wrought in the day— you in the night. I have had the applause of the crowd and the satisfaction that comes of being approved by the multitude, while the most that you have done has been witnessed by a few trembling, scarred, and foot-sore bondmen and women, whom you have led out of the house of bondage, and whose heartfelt "God bless you" has been your only reward. The midnight sky and the silent stars have been the witness of your devotion to freedom.

Part Three

☆☰☆☰☆☰☆☰☆☰☆☰☆☰☆☰☆

SOLDIERS
AND SPIES

☆☰☆☰☆☰☆☰☆☰☆☰☆☰☆☰☆☰☆☰☆☰☆☰☆☰☆

≋☆≋☆≋☆≋☆≋☆≋☆≋☆

CHAPTER 8

Belle Boyd

(1844–1900)

On Independence Day in 1861, Union soldiers pursuing General Jackson's Confederate Army marched into Martinsburg, Virginia (later West Virginia). As the men in blue occupied the town, pro-Union residents came out of their houses to celebrate. The crowd set off fireworks, sang "Yankee Doodle Dandy," and waved the American flag, which represented the Union during the war.

Meanwhile, Southern sympathizers—for the town was deeply divided—cowered in their houses. Word quickly spread through the town that some of the victorious Union soldiers, bent on revenge, were bashing in the windows of Southern sympathizers' homes.

The riled-up rioters decided to teach one particular rebel a lesson. At the home of pretty 17-year-old Belle Boyd, a known Confederate sympathizer, the rioters burst through the door. Then they pushed past the family and rushed upstairs to Belle's bedroom to tear down the Confederate flag that town folks said Belle had hung on her bedroom wall.

According to Belle's own telling of the episode, before the soldiers made it upstairs, a maid quickly removed the flag. Frustrated, the soldiers tramped back downstairs and announced they were going to hang the American flag from the family's roof. Outraged, Belle's mother

≋☆≋☆≋☆≋☆≋☆≋☆≋☆≋☆≋☆≋☆≋☆≋☆

stepped forward and declared: "Men, every member of this household will die before that flag is raised over us." In response, a red-faced soldier swore violently at Mrs. Boyd and pushed her aside. That was too much for the even more furious Belle, who drew her pistol and shot the soldier dead! Although the shooting was Belle's first and most violent exploit, it certainly wasn't her last. In fact, Belle was destined to become a Confederate superspy.

Born Maria Isabella Boyd in 1844, Belle spent her early years in the small village of Bunker Hill, near Martinsburg. Belle's father, Ben Boyd, managed a family farm and ran a country store. Lovely roses, silver maples, and honeysuckle vines surrounded the family's two-story home.

★≋★≋★≋★≋★≋★≋★≋★≋★≋★≋★≋★≋★≋★≋★≋

OLD GLORY, THE STARS AND BARS, AND THE SOUTHERN CROSS

The American flag, also called "Old Glory" and the "Stars and Stripes," represented the Union forces during the Civil War. It had thirteen alternating red and white stripes (for the original colonies) and white stars on a blue background in the upper left-hand corner. The number of stars changed depending on the number of states in the Union. (In February 1861, there were thirty-four stars.) In March 1861, the Confederacy adopted its own flag. At first, the "Stars and Bars" featured two red bars and one white bar and a circle of seven white stars in a blue box in the upper left-hand corner that symbolized the first states to secede. By July, the flag had thirteen stars, representing the seceding states (including Kentucky and Missouri, which had Confederate and Union governments). However, at the July 1861 Battle of Bull Run in Manassas, it was discovered that the new Confederate flag looked way too much like the Stars and Stripes when the generals had a hard time determining the position of their troops. That's when the South began using the "Southern Cross" as its battle flag. That flag featured a big blue X filled with thirteen white stars on a bright red background. It went through a few additional changes, but the basic design became the true symbol of the South.

★≋★≋★≋★≋★≋★≋★≋★≋★≋★≋★≋★≋★≋★≋★≋

Later, the family moved to the larger town of Martinsburg, where Ben opened another general store that did a brisk business.

Charming, confident Belle, the oldest of three children, got her way much of the time. Her parents were firm about some rules, however, including no children at dinner parties. By the time she was 12, that rule seemed horribly unfair to Belle. The day of one dinner party, she announced to her parents: "It's not right. I'm nearly an adult, and I want to attend." When her parents didn't budge, Belle stomped upstairs to bed—or so everyone thought.

Later that evening, when the Boyds' guests were preparing to go home, a horse suddenly pushed open the door and trotted in. From her perch on its back, Belle glared down at the guests and declared haughtily: "Well, my horse is old enough to attend, is he not?" Belle's stunned parents most likely would have scolded or punished their reckless daughter if one of the guests (later a Confederate officer) hadn't burst out laughing. "Surely so high a spirit should not be tamed," he cried. "I'm glad to meet your little rebel."

Shortly after that incident, Belle was shipped off to boarding school in Baltimore, Maryland (perhaps to settle her down!). Mount Washington Female College was a combined high school and college—and an innovative, experimental, and pricey place. The school founders believed that young ladies needed intellectual, physical, artistic, and domestic education. So Belle did daily physical exercises, dined on healthy fare that included very few sweets, and studied some serious subjects. Along with algebra, geography, government, and literature, Belle could choose music, singing, dancing, needlepoint, or French, among other things. About four years later, a world-wise, refined, and ladylike Belle was happily welcomed to the Boyd family dinner parties.

The teenage Belle had many admirers in Martinsburg. Young bachelors praised her figure, light blue eyes, golden-brown hair, and vivacious ways. Young Martinsburg girls expressed amazement (and envy) over her impossibly long eyelashes and vibrant red and green dresses.

However, some people didn't approve of Belle at all. One girl wondered if her lovely dresses weren't just a tad too tight, bright, and short. And more than one young gentleman commented (ladies were supposed to be modest and covered to their toes) that Belle had the daintiest ankles in the South. Clearly, the lively Belle was only *partly* reformed.

At age 16, Belle was most definitely ready for the next phase in her life—being formally introduced to society and entertaining suitors for her hand in marriage. At her debut ball, held in Washington, D.C., Belle wrote that she waltzed her way into the capital's high society "with high hopes and thoughtless joy." In the parties that followed, Belle wrote of hobnobbing with judges, congressmen, and even Secretary of War Floyd, who would soon leave the federal government to join the Confederacy.

Belle didn't only dance the night away, however. Her interest in the coming conflict led her to bend the rules of etiquette for ballroom conduct. Americans were rapidly choosing sides, and political talk crept into every corner of society, including ballrooms, which were once a place for lighthearted conversation only. Whenever possible, Belle slipped away to join clusters of men engaged in intense political discussions.

Belle's entrance into high society ended almost before it began, for President Abraham Lincoln took office in March 1861. A few weeks later, on April 11, Southerners attacked the federal Fort Sumter in South Carolina. Three days later, President Lincoln proclaimed "a state of insurrection" and called for 75,000 volunteers for three months.

In the South, Confederate leaders hustled to recruit a large army, too, and Belle learned that her father had joined General Thomas "Stonewall" Jackson's army encamped in Harper's Ferry, Virginia. Quickly, Belle joined thousands of Southern loyalists in fleeing Washington. The station was packed as Belle boarded a train bound for Martinsburg.

In Belle's home territory of northeastern Virginia, residents were deeply divided between the Union and the Confederacy. (So were people in the border states and other areas in the upper South). The divided loyalties led Virginia to split in two in 1863, with the new state of

West Virginia, including Martinsburg, siding with the North. The Boyd family, however, stood firmly with Dixie.

At home, Belle helped the rebel women of Martinsburg sew company flags with the motto: "Our God, our country, and our women." Then she and some girlfriends paid a visit to General Jackson's camp in nearby Harper's Ferry. At picnics and dances, Belle, the girls, and 5,000 new recruits had a gay old time. "A true woman always loves a soldier," Belle later gushed, "so many hearts were pledged." Belle's heart wasn't among them, however, unless you count General Jackson himself. Belle praised him as "a true apostle of Freedom."

In northeastern Virginia, Belle was in the thick of things, for both sides wanted control of the major railroads that intersected there. Towns like Harper's Ferry, Winchester, Strasburg, Front Royal, and Romney would be captured by the North one day, then lost to the South the next day. Martinsburg, in fact, changed hands thirty times!

ETIQUETTE OF THE BALLROOM: FROM ADVICE BOOKS OF THE DAY

- **Gentlemen must never ask a strange lady to dance, for that is insulting to her. He must apply to the master of ceremonies for a dance partner. If the lady is of an equal social position, the master will provide an introduction. If not, the master will choose a more suitable partner.**
- **Gentlemen and ladies should avoid long conversations.**
- **Gentlemen should never press a lady's waist while waltzing with her.**
- **Ladies must have the best seats and be protected and escorted at all times.**
- **Ladies can never be too particular in their conduct or too careful about their actions. Modesty should be the main characteristic of women—in dress, language, and manners.**
- **Ladies who give wanton glances earn their bad reputations. Many a young lady has lost a future husband by a wanton contempt for the rules.**
- **Ladies must behave as agreeably as possible at all times, giving gentlemen their undivided attention.**

In early July 1861, with fighting expected any day, Belle and her girl-friends left Harper's Ferry and hurried home to Martinsburg. Soon after that, Jackson's army met Union forces, fell back, and retreated through Martinsburg with 25,000 men in blue in hot pursuit.

While pursuing Jackson's men, the Union Army poured into, and occupied, Martinsburg. It was then, on Independence Day 1861, that Belle shot the Union soldier who dared to swear at her mother. After the shooting, irate Union soldiers surrounded the house, threatening to set it on fire. But Belle turned on the charm. She put away her pistol, dredged up some tears, and appealed for help to an officer sent from headquarters. The officer did Belle's bidding. He stopped the mob, investigated the shooting, and declared it self-defense. Not only did Belle get off scot-free, but Union guards were sent to protect the family!

Naturally, many Union officers wanted to meet the notorious Belle, and she delighted in the attention. Wisely, she gave up shooting Union men for captivating them. At dinners and dances with Union officers, she pretended to be a mindless ninny who didn't care whether a handsome man wore gray or blue. Meanwhile, she learned all she could about Union military plans and movements and secretly sent notes (via her maid) to two Confederate generals: Jeb Stuart and Stonewall Jackson.

The teenage spy career of Belle Boyd had begun, but knowing nothing of secret codes, disguised handwriting, and smuggling tech-niques made her a total amateur. Before long, a suspicious Union colonel got hold of a note in Belle's own handwriting and traced the source. The colonel called Belle into headquarters for questioning and issued a dire warning. "Spying is a serious offense," he informed Belle. "Do you know you could be sentenced to death?"

The colonel read Belle the Article of War (which recently had been amended to let military officials try and execute civilians without benefit of a civil trial). "Whosoever shall give food, ammunition, information or aid to the enemies of the U.S. government," the captain read, "shall suf-fer death, or other fit punishment." Belle listened politely until the colonel finished, then rose and curtsied low. Then, before sweeping out the door, she said sarcastically, "Thank you, gentlemen of the jury." From that hour on, the Union kept its eye on Belle. "All the mischief done to the Union cause was blamed on me," she later boasted. "And it is with joy and pride I confess they were usually right."

Despite the Union's suspicions, Belle managed to get away with a good

☆〰☆〰☆〰☆〰☆〰☆〰☆〰☆〰☆〰☆〰☆〰☆〰☆〰☆〰

ROSE GREENHOW: ANOTHER SUPERSPY

A forty-something mother of four, Rose Greenhow ran a hugely successful network of Confederate spies. Somehow Rose managed to learn of conversations in the White House and even found out where the president's guard was housed. Confederate President Jefferson Davis credited Rose with providing information that led to the South winning the July 1861 Battle of Bull Run in Manassas, Virginia. And Union General George McClellan complained: "She knew my plans. Four times I've had to change them!"

ROSE GREENHOW AND HER DAUGHTER IN OLD CAPITAL PRISON.

In August 1861, Union officials caught Rose red-handed and put her under house arrest in her Washington, D.C., home. Amazingly, she managed to keep running her spy ring from captivity but was soon caught and sent (with her 8-year-old daughter) to Old Capital Prison for several months.

In 1864, Rose toured Europe in a last-ditch effort to drum up support for the Confederates. While abroad, she published *My Imprisonment and the First Year of Abolition Rule in Washington*, in which she ranted about the sins of the North. The book sold quite well, Rose's fame spread, and soon Queen Victoria of England and Napoleon III of France wanted to meet her. She also got herself engaged to an earl!

Rose never had a chance to marry, however, for she drowned while attempting to return to the United States on a British ship. To avoid capture by a Union gunboat pursuing the ship, Rose and some other men fled in a rowboat, which capsized. Although the men made it safely to shore, Rose's heavy skirts and cloak, plus hidden dispatches and gold coins, pulled her down.

〰☆〰☆〰☆〰☆〰☆〰☆〰☆〰☆〰☆〰☆〰☆〰☆〰☆〰☆〰☆

bit of spying. It helped that Colonel Turner Ashby, the head of military scouts in the Shenandoah Valley, showed Belle how to be more crafty and careful. Soon she knew the secrets of spies, from writing in code and donning clever disguises, to hiding messages in watches, shoes, and hair buns.

Belle's lucky streak ran out, however, in March 1862. At the Winchester, Virginia, railroad station, Union detectives (undercover officers who went after spies) placed her under arrest. As unruffled as ever, Belle merely straightened her hat, smiled, and acted as if it were a great joke. In a way, it was, too. For Belle's punishment was being "imprisoned" in a comfortable Baltimore hotel for only a week; then she was released with yet another warning!

This wasn't the first or the last time that male gallantry would be Belle's best weapon. Blinded by the notion that females could not possibly do much harm, officials often let female spies go with fatherly warnings. Belle and other women spies took full advantage of the manners of the day, especially that a true gentleman should never be harsh to a lady. Because of such beliefs, Belle would be arrested several times, then quickly released.

Rather than slowing her down, Belle's arrests seemed to make her more daring than ever. From Baltimore, she traveled to her aunt's hotel in Union-held Front Royal, Virginia. Union officers had taken over the hotel, evicting her aunt and uncle to a small cottage out back. Yet instead of being dismayed, Belle smelled opportunity. She set about charming both junior officers and the commander in charge, General James Shields. Instead of trying to convince them that she was suddenly a diehard Union supporter, Belle simply acted like a fun-loving woman out for a good time—with gallant gentlemen of all political persuasions. One of Belle's conquests confided to her that top officers would soon meet in the hotel dining room to plan battle strategies.

Determined to learn more, Belle hid herself in a closet on the night of the meeting. She enlarged a hole in the floor, eavesdropped on the officers, and memorized much of the information. The rest she wrote down in code. When the meeting ended, Belle saddled a horse, grabbed

one of her handy phony passes (which allowed her to get through to Confederate territory), and headed straight to Confederate-held territory. Union sentries stopped Belle twice, but let her through when she waved the pass in front of them and talked nervously about a sick family member needing her at home. At last, Belle delivered her message and made it back safely to Front Royal.

Several weeks later, Belle made her most daring delivery. On May 23, 1862, Belle looked out her window in Front Royal to see Union soldiers swarming through the streets. Naturally, she hit the streets, too, pretending to be worried about the Confederates' approach. Belle asked passing soldiers what was happening and learned that Generals Jackson and Ewell had surprised the small Union force holding Martinsburg, and were only a mile or so from town. Union soldiers were quickly removing stored weapons and ammunition so that these materials would not be seized; then they planned to draw back to Winchester, burning the bridges as they crossed. Once in Winchester, the unit planned to join with several larger armies and converge on Jackson's rebel army.

Belle knew it was critical that General Jackson know what was going on in Martinsburg. If the Confederates marched into town quickly, they might capture the weapons and keep the Union from fleeing and burning the bridge. With binoculars, Belle located the Confederates' position nearly a mile away. Then she rushed downstairs, grabbed a white bonnet, and raced toward the Confederates. Scrambling across fences and fields, Belle tried to stay between the hills, out of sight of the Union sentries.

According to Belle's own account, as she came to open ground between the Union and Confederate troops, there was nowhere to hide. The Union sentries spied Belle and the bullets rained down, kicking up the dust as she ran. One ripped through Belle's skirt, and she sprinted ahead to get beyond the sentries' range. When Belle made it far enough so that the flabbergasted rebels could see her face, she fell to her knees, exhausted. Then she pulled off her white bonnet and waved it toward the town while shouting: "Press on. Press on!"

General Jackson sent Major Harry Douglass forward to question

Belle. In his memoirs, the major recalled Belle as a "tall, supple and graceful" figure with flushed cheeks and shining eyes. Belle told the major that the Yankee force was small and he should charge right down. "I must hurry back," she added quickly. "My love to all the dear boys— and remember if you meet me in town, you haven't seen me today."

General Jackson already suspected some of the information provided by Belle, yet she confirmed it. The Confederates took Martinsburg, saved the bridge from burning, then took Front Royal and pushed toward the nation's capital. To keep Jackson from taking Washington, D.C., the panicked Union was forced to pull back men from an assault on Richmond. A couple of days later, General Jackson sent Belle a note that read: "I thank you, for myself and for the Army, for the immense service that you have rendered your country. Hastily, I am your friend, T. J. Jackson, C.S.A." Belle treasured that note until her dying day.

For a week after Belle's exploit, newspapers ran stories calling her a "sensation in the whole village" and a "notorious spy." One story even told of the sword-wielding "La Belle Rebelle" leading the Confederate charge into Martinsburg! A week later, Belle was arrested but claimed it was a case of mistaken identity. Some other girl had run through that field, she insisted, not her. The Yankees let her go but decided to spring a trap that she couldn't get out of so easily.

A handsome Union spy named C. W. Smitley was assigned to give Belle a taste of her own medicine. Smitley posed as a paroled Confederate soldier, captured by the Union but allowed to stay in the town. He ran into Belle at a dinner party and swept her off her feet. Standing by the piano, C. W. and Belle crooned "The Bonnie Blue Flag." In the moonlight, they cuddled and sparked (an old-fashioned word for kissing). They saw a great deal of each other, and for the first time, a young man captured Belle's heart.

Belle also trusted C. W. completely. In July 1862, when he said the Yankees were deporting him to the South, Belle leaned close and asked him to carry a secret message to General Jackson. C. W. agreed. But while Belle dreamed innocently of romance, the bare-faced liar of a boyfriend went straight to the Union secretary of war and presented his ironclad evidence against Belle. In short order, Union detectives descended on Belle's house like vultures, rifling through her clothing and confiscating her pistol and papers. After finding even more evidence against her, the detectives hauled Belle off to the Old Capital Prison in Washington, D.C.

At the prison, Belle got her own cell, with a view of Pennsylvania Avenue and the fine homes where she'd once been a belle of the ball. Union officials soon marched in to question Belle and pressure her to sign an oath of allegiance to the United States. "I hope when I commence that oath, my tongue may cleave to the roof of my mouth," Belle huffed. "I hope before I swear allegiance that my arm falls paralyzed to my side." Belle's enemies soon realized she'd never crack and let her get on with entertaining herself. One visitor who came to visit the prison's most famous inmate found her reading *Harper's* magazine and eating peaches! "I can afford to stay here as long as Stanton (the secretary of war) wants to keep me," she boasted.

The solitary confinement might have gotten to Belle if she hadn't found ways to communicate with other prisoners. She passed messages by tying them around marbles, which she rolled through the bars to other prisoners. She tucked other notes into hollow rubber balls and threw them out the window to a friend outside the prison walls. She also sang Southern songs to cheer other Confederate prisoners and irritate the guards. Belle drove pro-Union guards and prisoners in the jail crazy by singing such lines as "She spurns the Northern scum!" at the top of her lungs.

One prison experience, which Belle later left out of her memoirs, involved another romance. According to other prisoners and the warden, Belle became engaged to the Confederate prisoner in the cell across from hers, Lieutenant McVay (his first name is unknown). The superintendent, who had become a friend of Belle's, was so pleased with the engagement that he bought her a trousseau—a bride's new wardrobe. Then he shipped it to Richmond, where Belle picked it up in early 1863, after she was freed in a prisoner exchange.

Once in Richmond, Belle never saw McVay again, at least as far as anyone knows. He wasn't released with her, and in fact he simply disappeared from the public record. Perhaps his love had cooled, or maybe hers had. Or maybe the engagement had been Belle's tricky way of getting a fine new wardrobe paid for by her jailer. No one knows for certain, but one thing is sure: When Richmond rolled out the welcome carpet for their beloved spy, Belle didn't seem heartbroken. And she certainly was wearing some fancy new clothes.

In the Confederate capital, Belle basked in the admiration that came her way, then spent a few months traveling through the South. But by July 1863, she was back in Confederate-held Martinsburg when the Union captured the town once again. Secretary of War Stanton definitely did not want Belle loose in his territory, so off she went to prison again.

At "fetid and foul" Carroll Prison, also in Washington, D.C., Belle was held with "rebels, prisoners of state, hostages, blockade-runners, smugglers, desperadoes, spies, criminals under sentence of death, and, lastly, a large number of federal officers convicted of defrauding the government." Again, Belle managed to cause trouble. Somehow, she smuggled a Confederate flag into her cell and dangled it out the window. "Take in that flag, or I'll blow your brains out!" a guard yelled. When Belle ignored the command, the guard did indeed shoot at her—but his aim was poor and he missed!

After a few months of relentless lobbying by Belle's father—and because she grew ill with typhoid—Belle was released again. This time, she decided it might be wise to head to England for "a rest." Actually, toward the end of the war, lots of Confederates developed a sudden, burning need to take a foreign vacation. After all, the South was rapidly losing, and no one knew what punishments the victorious Yankees might dish out to their former enemies. English society (with its many Southern sympathizers) seemed a lot more welcoming to many ex-spies and Confederate leaders.

Not that the Confederate leadership was ready to admit defeat in early 1864, when Belle began planning to bolt. The armies kept fighting, and rebel spies kept smuggling messages to England, pleading for military aid that would never arrive. (England had stayed neutral during the Civil War, but Southern leaders kept hoping that would change.) According to Belle's memoir, Jefferson Davis himself heard of Belle's voyage and asked her to carry one of those desperate last-minute dispatches to England. Being the loyal lady that she was, Belle of course agreed.

In May 1864, using the name Mrs. Lewis, Belle sailed on the *Greyhound* from Wilmington, North Carolina, to England. Along with Belle and her messages, the tall sailing ship carried tons of Southern cotton that would be sold in England. To get to the open ocean, however, the *Greyhound* had to sneak past Union warships that lined the coast. Under the cover of darkness, the ship crept out to sea, but as dawn broke the U.S.S. *Connecticut* came into view. The Union gunboat sighted the *Greyhound,* sped toward it, and began firing. Belle wrote that as the crew threw cotton bales overboard to make the ship sail faster, she burned her secret messages and tossed $25,000 in gold and Confederate bills into the ocean. Meanwhile, the Union ship drew closer and soon captured the *Greyhound.*

The Union installed a young ensign, Samuel Hardinge, to sail the captured crew and ship to Boston (with stops along the way in Virginia and New York). Sam made eyes at Belle, who made eyes back. "I saw at a glance he was made of other stuff than his comrades," Belle gushed. "His dark brown hair hung down on his shoulders; his eyes were large and bright. His every movement was so much that of a refined gentleman." Love blossomed, but that didn't get in the way of Belle helping the *Greyhound*'s original rebel captain to escape.

By the time the ship had docked in Boston, in late 1864, newspapers had gotten wind of Belle's true identity and her shipboard romance. Newspaper writers followed the by-then-engaged Belle and Sam everywhere and wrote romantic stories about them. One even dubbed Belle the "Cleopatra of the Confederacy."

Instead of arresting Belle, Union officials banished her to Canada—this time with a written warning that if she entered the United States again, she would be shot. From Canada, Belle sailed to England, while

Sam asked the navy for a leave of absence to join her and marry her. Instead, the navy launched an inquiry into Sam's role in letting the shipboard captain escape.

According to Belle, the navy didn't find enough evidence to charge Sam with any crime but did dismiss him from the navy. (However, he may have deserted, as you'll soon see.) Sam joined Belle in London, and on August 25, 1864, the couple were married at St. James Church in Piccadilly. The London newspapers paid homage to the blushing bride, and back in America, the poet Carl Sandburg fumed: "She should have been convicted and shot at sunrise based on the evidence against her."

What happened next muddies the waters of Belle's (and Sam's) story. Belle stayed in England, expecting a child, while Sam returned alone to America. Belle insisted that Sam had gone back to see her family and "clear his name." Sam was never disloyal to the Union at all, she said. However, the navy had another view, for Sam was arrested and jailed for desertion.

In London, Belle was worried to death and broke. To raise money and pay for her rooms in the Brunswick Hotel, she had to sell her jewelry and wedding presents. To win sympathy for Sam—and earn more money—Belle wrote her memoirs. Before she published them, however, she wrote a remarkable letter to Abraham Lincoln. In it she offered not to publish the book *if* Sam was set free.

Lincoln did not reply to Belle's letter, and there's no reason to think he paid it much mind. But Sam was released in February 1865, a month before the book was published in London. *Belle Boyd in Camp and Prison* sold well in England and gave Belle a chance to give one last plug for her beloved South. She wrote: "I firmly believe that in this fiery ordeal, in this suffering, misery, and woe, the South is but undergoing purification by fire and steel that will, in good time, and by God's decree, work out her own independence."

Soon Belle had other things on her mind than the resurrection of Dixie, however. According to her, Sam returned to London but died of an illness a few months later (this is debatable though, and he might have just quietly disappeared). Belle took advantage of her celebrity status and launched a career as an actress. In 1866, she made her debut in *The Lady of Lyons* in Manchester, England. In 1868, she appeared on the New York stage in *The Honeymoon.* Belle also gave lectures about her wartime experiences.

During her years as an actress, Belle found steady work, but the roles grew smaller as she grew older. She married at least two more times and had four (or perhaps more) children. In 1900, while performing in Kilbourne, Wisconsin, Belle had a heart attack and died. Her beloved South was far away, and there was no money to pay for a lavish funeral. But the kind Yankees of Kilbourne sprang for a coffin and grave site, and four Civil War veterans carried her to her grave. One former Confederate soldier in the area put up a tombstone that proudly read: "Belle Boyd: Confederate Spy."

FROM BELLE BOYD TO PRESIDENT LINCOLN, JANUARY 24, 1865

Dear Sir,

I have heard from good authority that if I suppress the Book I have now ready for publication, you may be induced to consider leniently the case of my husband, S. Wylde Hardinge, now a prisoner in Fort Delaware. I think it would be well for you & me to come to some definite understanding— My Book was not originally intended to be more than a personal narrative, but since my husband's unjust arrest I have made it political, & introduced many atrocious circumstances respecting your Government. . . . If you will release my husband & set him free, so that he may join me here in England by the beginning of March, I pledge you my word that my Book shall be suppressed. Should my husband not be with me by the 25th of March I shall at once place my Book in the hands of a publisher.

Trusting an immediate reply,

I am Sir, Yr. obdt. Servant, Belle Boyd Hardinge

Pauline Cushman

(1 8 3 3 – 1 8 9 3)

Harriet Wood, who later adopted the stage name Pauline Cushman, was born in 1833 in cosmopolitan New Orleans, Louisiana. When she was small, her parents moved to the Michigan frontier, and Harriet grew up a country girl—but a reluctant one! As a young girl, she decided to someday escape the boondocks and become an actress on the big-city stage. And at age 18, that's just what Harriet did. With great determination and a little luck, she realized her dream, becoming not only an actress but also a celebrated spy.

We know little about Pauline's early life, but we do know that at age 18 she was hired as an actress by Thomas Placide's Varieties stage company in New Orleans. The stage company had a permanent theater in New Orleans but also toured the United States, east of the Mississippi. The gypsy-like existence of the touring company took Pauline from stages in small town music halls to ritzy Broadway theaters. For the first several years, Pauline got only small parts—and led a very rough life.

Pauline, like most actresses, ignored public disapproval. She also put up with long hours of rehearsal, carrying all her own baggage, staying in seedy boardinghouses, and getting pitiful pay. Determined to rise above it all and achieve stardom, Pauline set about proving she could steal the show. To be a star, she had to have many talents. She had to be able to perform in comedies and tragedies. She had to sing well, dance well, and work her fanny off. And she had to be endlessly charming to fans who lingered after the shows to wine and dine the performers.

By the late 1850s, Pauline had proven she had what it took to make it big in the grueling theater world. She still had to rise at 9 A.M.,

ADAH MENKEN'S COSTUMES SCANDALIZED RESPECTABLE SOCIETY, BUT AUDIENCES LOVED HER.

ADAH ISAACS MENKEN

Respectable men and women looked down their noses at actresses during the nineteenth century because it was considered a very brazen and unladylike profession. One of the most fascinating actresses of Civil War times was Adah Isaacs Menken, who, like Pauline Cushman, was born in New Orleans. Adah told so many wild stories about her background that none are reliable, but historians think her real (and quite exotic) name might have been Philomène Croi Théodore. She was Jewish and may also have been part African American, French, and/or Native American.

It was said that Adah's performances could make men weep. Often they raised many a respectable eyebrow, too. In one Broadway production, Adah cut her hair short and played Hamlet. In another, she charged onto the stage on horseback, in a scandalous, skin-colored leotard and tights. She also sang, danced, wrote poetry, and painted.

Sadly, Adah died of tuberculosis at age 33. During her last years, spent in Paris, she published a book of poetry and befriended the writers Mark Twain, Walt Whitman, and Charles Dickens. Before her death, she visited with her rabbi and wrote to a friend: "I am lost to art and life. Yet, when all is said and done, have I not at my age tasted more of life than most women who live to be a hundred?"

rehearse for several hours, and perform in shows until midnight. But at least there were rewards for all that hard work! As a leading lady, Pauline got starring roles, earned great money, wore gorgeous gowns, and stayed in elegant hotel rooms. Everywhere she went, a pack of photographers and journalists followed.

Sometime in the 1850s, Pauline married a musician, Charles Dickenson, and had two children. Like most theater couples (actresses often married managers, musicians, or other actors), they took their children, Charles II and Ida, on the road. However, according to Pauline's biographer both children died young (it's not clear when) of diphtheria, a childhood illness for which there was no cure at the time.

When the Civil War began in 1861, Charles joined the Union as a member of a regimental band. A year later, he died of dysentery (an illness brought on by poor sanitation in army camps). Pauline sided firmly with the Union. However, she kept her feelings hidden because her livelihood depended on her being liked by everyone, no matter what their views. Pauline's neutral behavior changed in May 1863, however, and in a very unusual way!

In Union-held Louisville, Kentucky, Pauline was performing at Wood's Theater when some Southern officers (captured by the Union, but allowed to live in town) took in Pauline's show. When the show ended, the soldiers treated Pauline to a late supper and pressed her about whether she supported the North or the South. Not wanting to upset her fans, Pauline implied to the rebel lads that she had nothing against the South. The soldiers teased Pauline more, though, telling her that to *prove* her loyalty to their side she should stop in the middle of her next performance and offer a toast to Confederate President Jefferson Davis! To the rebels' surprise, Pauline agreed, for on the spot, she'd hatched a secret plan.

Pauline's plan was to convince the Confederates she was on their side—then spy for the Union! After the soldiers left Pauline, she secretly contacted Colonel Moore, the Union's provost marshall of Louisville, and laid out her scheme. The colonel happily entered into Pauline's conspiracy, and the next evening, Pauline stopped in the middle of the performance and belted out: "Here's to Jeff Davis and the Confederacy. May the South always maintain her honor and her rights!"

The toast brought the house down—with some audience members booing and hissing and others cheering. As Pauline had expected, the theater manager (who had to stay on the good side of Union authorities) cut Pauline from the show. Soon the authorities arrived, led by Colonel Moore, who arrested Pauline. Of course, Pauline went nowhere near a jail cell. Instead, in a private location she recited an oath of loyalty as a member of the secret service.

Pauline was smuggled into Confederate territory in June 1863 and began using a cover story that she was searching for her brother, a miss-

UNION SPIES: ELIZABETH VAN LEW AND MARY BOWSER

The dynamic Elizabeth Van Lew and her servant, Mary Bowser, spied for the Union, too. Elizabeth, a Richmond native and fervent abolitionist, worked hard to establish a reputation of being a nut. "Crazy Bett" traveled by mule, praised the Union loudly, and muttered loudly to herself in public. Then she went to Libby Prison for Union soldiers and asked permission to visit. The first Confederate officer she talked to said: "What are you, crazy? You can't nurse those men. I know people who would be glad to shoot the lot of them."

Elizabeth stuck to her guns, muttering away until she got permission. Then she began taking clothes, bedding, and medicine to the Union prisoners. Also, right under the rebels' noses, Elizabeth was smuggling information in and out and helping to plan escapes.

Consorting with the enemy got Elizabeth shunned by Richmond society, and spying became more difficult. Undaunted, she enlisted the help of Mary, her African American servant. Mary managed to get herself hired by President Jefferson Davis and eavesdropped on important meetings in the Confederate White House!

ing Confederate soldier. When Confederate troops traveled through Kentucky and Tennessee (also called "the Cumberland"), Pauline was close behind. She gathered information about troop strength and battle plans, then passed it on through a network of Union spies.

For a couple of months, Pauline provided good information, but Confederate authorities got suspicious. In Shelbyville, Tennessee, soldiers came to a farmhouse where Pauline was staying and searched her belongings. Pauline hadn't had time to pass on a map she'd stolen from a Confederate Army engineer and had tucked it into her boots. The soldiers discovered the map, arrested Pauline, and housed her in a tent under guard until she could be transported to higher officers. Immediately, Pauline tried to dig a hole under her tent to escape but was caught before she got away.

Despite her foiled escape, Pauline showed no fear. The guards ushered her into the tent of the notorious Confederate Colonel John Morgan. (Morgan's unit—the Kentucky Rifles—operated apart from the regular army; the men hid in mountain caves, cutting telegraph lines, stealing horses, committing murder, and otherwise terrorizing Yankees and Yankee supporters in the area). Pauline tried to bluff her way out of trouble. "I am a true and innocent daughter of the South!" Pauline huffed. Although too wily to be convinced, the dashing colonel found Pauline's bravado charming. More wining and dining followed, during which John Morgan (also called Jack) gave Pauline a silver revolver and a diamond ring!

After showering Pauline with gifts, Colonel Morgan reluctantly escorted her to his superior, General Nathan Forrest. Forrest was in the middle of a card game when Colonel Morgan walked in arm in arm with his pretty captive. The general looked up at Pauline briefly and said: "I've been looking for you a

THE UNION MADE PAULINE AN HONORARY CAVALRY MAJOR AND GAVE HER A SPIFFY RIDING HABIT MODELED AFTER A UNION UNIFORM.

long time, but I have got this last shuffle, so you'll have to wait." Pauline waited impatiently as Jack reluctantly bid her good-bye. "I hope we meet again," he said, "and that I have something better to feed you than bread baked in ashes and rot gut whiskey."

To the general, Pauline passionately denied her guilt once again. "T'is a false charge, and I would like to send a bullet through the man who makes it!" she cried. "I am a poor refugee expelled from Union lines because of my strong Southern feeling."

The general boomed: "Well, you're certainly made of good fighting stuff for a woman." Then he fobbed her off on yet another higher-up, General Bragg in Shelbyville, Tennessee. At his headquarters, Bragg accused Pauline of having a Northern accent, and she declared it was from playing Yankee roles on stage. Then Bragg said she'd most likely be hanged, to which Pauline remarked: "I won't be terribly useful to anyone dangling at the end of a rope!"

Pauline's thoughts didn't interest General Bragg, who sentenced her to hang and locked her up to await that fate. But Pauline got sick (or conned her captors into believing she was sick), and it was considered terribly bad manners to hang a sick person. So the rebels plunked Pauline in the infirmary until she was well enough to die.

Before execution day arrived, though, Pauline was saved. Union bugles sounded outside, General Bragg's army of Tennessee fled, and soon Union officers and Pauline were celebrating together. When President Lincoln learned of her narrow escape, he made Pauline an honorary cavalry major. With the honor came a spiffy riding habit modeled after a Union uniform.

After Pauline's dramatic liberation, Union newspapers hailed her as a heroine. The *New York Times* reported that "no woman had suffered more or rendered more service to the Federal cause than Pauline Cushman, the female scout and spy." Many stories exaggerated Pauline's exploits, saying she'd worn many disguises, including men's clothes, and wielded a pistol fearlessly.

Such attention blew Pauline's cover, and she traded her spy glass for a stint as a Civil War celebrity. At the P. T. Barnum Museum in New York City, she gave lectures billed as "Pauline Cushman: Spy of the Cumberland." Musicians played patriotic songs as Pauline marched across the stage in a uniform, regaling audiences with both true and tall tales of her adventures. In 1865, a publisher turned the notes for her lectures into a book called *The Life of Pauline Cushman, the Celebrated Union Spy and Scout,* which drew rave reviews. Happily, Pauline took off for a lecture tour of the American West.

The lively West suited Pauline, and in the 1870s she moved there. After running an Arizona hotel for a couple of years, Pauline moved to California, where she married the theater manager August Fichtner and gave lectures around Santa Cruz. When one newspaper poked fun at the aging spy—and even doubted her identity—Pauline threatened to horsewhip the editor!

By the late 1870s, Pauline's second husband had died, and she began to suffer from arthritis and rheumatism. In 1879, she returned briefly to Arizona, where she married a sheriff named Jere Fryer. But the marriage didn't last, and Pauline returned to San Francisco to work as a housekeeper and maid. In 1893, she died in a run-down boardinghouse after overdosing on morphine, the highly addictive drug that was often prescribed for pain. Some people believed Pauline committed suicide, but the coroner ruled that she had been taking morphine as medicine and overdosed accidentally.

Because she was penniless, Pauline was headed for an unmarked pauper's grave, but her fans refused to let that happen. They arranged a funeral that drew more than 800 Civil War veterans—and hundreds of bouquets and wreaths of flowers. When Pauline was buried with military honors in the National Military Cemetery in San Francisco, grizzled Union veterans carried her to her grave.

Loreta Janeta Velázquez

(1 8 4 2 – ?)

The exotic Cuban-French-American beauty Loreta Janeta Velázquez was a daredevil damsel who swapped her broom for a musket and became a Confederate soldier. She was also an enthusiastic embellisher (exaggerator), so what we know about her is part fact, part fiction.

Loreta was born in 1842 and grew up on a Cuban plantation. According to Loreta, her wealthy family boasted such ancestors as Don Diego Velázquez, the first governor of Cuba, and Don Diego Rodriguez Velázquez, a great Spanish artist. Loreta's mother was half American and half French, and may have been from New Orleans, which is where the family sent Loreta to live when she was a young teenager.

In the multicultural melting pot of New Orleans, Spanish, French, African, and European cultures mingled. Loreta lived with a strict aunt and attended a Catholic girls' school. But despite this sheltered home life, Loreta was exposed to new ideas that inspired her later adventures. In school, after learning about the French heroine and soldier Joan of Arc, Loreta also dressed up as a boy. Then she snuck out of the house to try out her disguise, which no one saw through.

At school, Loreta was influenced by her American classmates. They insisted that girls should be allowed to love and marry anyone they wanted—something that wasn't at all accepted in Loreta's Spanish-influenced household. In fact, Loreta's father, Don Velázquez, had already engaged her to a boy named Raphael.

At first, Loreta liked her fiancé, but at age 14, she fell hard for an American soldier named William. (Last names often weren't used in Loreta's memoir.) William had many strikes against him. He wasn't Spanish or Catholic—and he wasn't Raphael. And he was an *American* soldier. (Don Velázquez wasn't too fond of American soldiers, for he'd taken the side of Mexico in the 1840s, when that nation had fought the United States over control of the Southwest.)

When Loreta's father got wind of the romance, he hit the roof. Along with refusing to allow Loreta to marry William, Don Velázquez threatened to never speak to Loreta again or give the couple any financial support. Ignoring this threat, the young couple eloped in 1856. They were poor but happy, and Don Velázquez eventually accepted the marriage.

For Loreta, discovering the difficulties of being a soldier's wife was harder than putting up with her father's wrath. Because William was on active duty, he only came home on leave once in a while, and Loreta was mostly left alone. This lonely life continued for the next several years, during which Loreta had three children. When all of the children died as infants, Loreta's grief and loneliness grew.

By the time the Civil War began, Loreta's restlessness spurred her to take a dramatic step—one most people would have considered crazy. Once again, she would dress in male clothing and fool the world. But this time, she'd dress as a soldier—and fight as one, too.

According to Loreta's memoirs (some historians believe Loreta exaggerated this part), she claimed to have confided her daring plan to William when he came home on leave. Not surprisingly, William said it was the most ridiculous thing he'd ever heard. "A refined and delicate lady should not be among the rough company of men," he said. When

WOMEN SOLDIERS OF THE CIVIL WAR

SARAH EDMONDS (A.K.A. FRANK THOMPSON) SERVED TWO YEARS IN THE UNION ARMY AND WAS NEVER DISCOVERED. LATER, SHE RECEIVED A MILITARY PENSION.

At least 400 women are known to have dressed as men and served as soldiers during the war (399 more than during the American Revolution). Several of them later wrote memoirs, which helped convince the public that women might not be such shrinking violets after all.

Jennie Hodges (who in 1844 came to America from Ireland after stowing away on a ship) called herself Albert Cashier and fought with the Illinois Volunteer Infantry. Her comrades said she was small, quiet, likable, and brave. After the war, Jennie (Albert) stayed in her disguise and worked as a handyman. Only after she broke her leg at age 66 did a doctor discover that "he" was a she. The doctor kept Jennie's secret, though, and so did the people at the Soldiers' and Sailors' Home in Quincy, where she spent her last years.

Unlike Jennie, most females disguised as soldiers went back to a traditional female life after the war. Sarah Edmonds (called Frank Thompson) married and had three children. Explaining her wartime adventures, she said: "I was naturally fond of adventure and a little ambitious, a good deal romantic. But patriotism was the true secret of my success."

★☰★☰★☰★☰★☰★☰★☰★☰★☰★☰★☰★☰★☰★☰★☰

Loreta begged to differ, William decided to give her a taste of the male existence. Loreta braided her hair tight, put on a wig and false mustache, bound her chest, and put on one of William's suits. Then the couple hit the town for a night of manly carousing with William's army buddies.

On her excursion to the saloons, Loreta found the men's "vile" language shocking, their manners "revolting," and their tall tales amusing.

★☰★☰★☰★☰★☰★☰★☰★☰★☰★☰★☰★☰★☰★☰★☆

Yet Loreta also was drawn to the "brotherhood of men," much to her husband's dismay. By evening's end, in fact, Loreta wanted to join their ranks more than ever. "I was perfectly wild on the subject," she wrote.

Because William was dead set against Loreta's crazy plan, she gave in (or at least appeared to). But after William joined the Confederacy and marched off to Virginia, she again donned her manly duds. According to Loreta's memoir, she visited a tailor's shop, deepened her voice, and ordered two Confederate lieutenant's uniforms. When the tailor looked at her suspiciously, Loreta almost panicked. But the tailor just shook his head and said: "Ah, what you want to go to war for? You are too young for the fighting. What will your mother say?"

LORETA CUT A
FINE FIGURE IN
HER CONFEDERATE
UNIFORM.

Although Loreta was relieved, the experience convinced her that she needed to beef up her disguise. So Loreta built a man-shaped frame out of wire and padding and wore it underneath her clothing. She hacked off her long black hair and firmly glued on the false mustache. She also practiced spitting between her teeth.

Once satisfied she could pass as a man, Loreta decided on a new name, Harry T. Buford. Then she journeyed into Arkansas posing as a recruiter for the Confederacy. After rounding up a group of fresh fish—army slang for new recruits—Loreta writes that she marched them to Virginia and sought out her husband. Then with a grand flourish, she turned the recruits over to him before revealing her true identity.

Loreta writes that her husband was first shocked but then thrilled—so thrilled that he totally changed his mind and fully supported her cross-dressing masquerade. Although it's a great yarn, this part of Loreta's story probably is made up or exaggerated. We know this because she also said William died a couple of days later in an accident, but army records suggest he died after the war. Whatever happened, he was no longer in the picture, and Loreta was free to continue her adventures.

Rather than enlisting in a regiment, Loreta remained an irregular, offering her services to whatever group of Confederates needed an extra gun. Both the Union and the Confederacy encouraged men who hadn't volunteered or weren't drafted—forced by law to serve—to be "irregulars" or "independents" who lent their services to the "regular" army as needed.

As an irregular, Loreta traveled from battle to battle for the next two years, never losing her nerve. Yet between fights, she would often go back to dressing as a woman. Holed up in a comfortable hotel, she'd "renew her spirit."

Loreta's experiences at Bull Run, Ball's Bluff, Fort Donelson, and Shiloh soon changed her rose-colored view of war. She fought off swarms of gallinippers (mosquitoes) and dined on ironclad possum (armadillo). She captured prisoners and dug trenches. She dodged bullets and shot them. She knew bloodthirsty rage, the thrill of victory, and crushing depression. In 1862, during stints with frontier units in Ohio, Kentucky, and Tennessee, the battles were so ugly that she considered quitting. "I fully realized what a fearful thing this human slaughtering was," she wrote.

For most soldiers, a favorite form of relief from the horrors of war was romancing damsels who lived near camp. In the beginning, Loreta went with her pals to dances and parties—and got a great kick out of bashful, blushing maidens falling head over heels in love with her. In fact, Loreta at first thought it was great fun to string the girls along even to the point of getting engaged to them! In time, however, she began to feel a little guilty about breaking hearts, so she began flashing a photograph of a fake fiancée to keep the ladies at bay.

In 1863, Loreta was wounded slightly and returned to Confederate-held New Orleans to heal. This time, she chose to remain in her male disguise, and some people grew suspicious. Someone decided that Harry T. Buford was really a female—and a *Union* spy!

Loreta was arrested and hauled before the mayor, who decided she was indeed a woman. "Go and change your clothes, right now," the mayor ordered. Stubbornly, Loreta said: "Sir, prove that I am a woman. When you do that, you can order me to change my dress." Any hope

Loreta had of bluffing her way into a prompt discharge quickly died, however. The mayor just ordered her jailed in the "calaboose" until a doctor could examine her. At that, Loreta spilled the beans. "I am a woman but no spy," she told the mayor. Instead of praise, the mayor threw Loreta in jail for ten days and fined her $10.

Loreta continued her charade through the war and afterward married at least two more times. She also traveled through the West and spent some time at a colony of ex-Confederates in Venezuela. In 1876, the widowed Loreta was living in New York with a small child and badly in need of funds. So she wrote the book from which we get her story (after 1876, the record of her life ends). Never one to mince words, Loreta admitted in her introduction that she wrote her memoir—*The Woman in Battle: A Narrative of the Exploits, Adventures, and Travels of Madame Loreta Janeta Velázquez, Otherwise Known as Lieutenant Harry T. Buford, Confederate States Army*—to earn money, not to earn praise or adoration. "I am philosophical enough," she wrote, "to get along without that."

CATHY WILLIAMS: BUFFALO SOLDIER

Cathy Williams, an ex-slave from Missouri, is the only African American woman known to have served as a soldier with America's first African American troops. During the war, Cathy, in female dress, worked as a paid cook traveling with the Union Army in Arkansas, Louisiana, Missouri, and Virginia. Not until after the war did she dress as a man, change her name to William Cathay, and join the African American infantry. (Native American tribes on the western plains dubbed the black units "buffalo soldiers" for their bravery and black curly hair.)

Cathy served with the 38th Infantry in New Mexico and successfully hid her secret for two years. Then she was foiled by sickness, like so many women soldiers. After Cathy got smallpox, she was hospitalized, and doctors discovered her true sex. The army discharged her, and later Cathy told a reporter why she'd wanted to be a soldier. "I wanted to make my own living and not be dependent on relations or friends," she explained.

Part Four

☆☰☆☰☆☰☆☰☆☰☆☰☆☰☆

THE FIRST
LADIES

☆☰☆☰☆☰☆☰☆☰☆☰☆☰☆☰☆☰☆☰☆☰☆☰☆

Mary Todd Lincoln

(1 8 1 8 – 1 8 8 2)

Mary Todd Lincoln pushed her husband, Abe, to become president, sent White House goodies to wounded soldiers, and found jobs for runaway slaves. The first lady of the land also was a shopaholic who held séances in the White House! While many wished Mary would act like a sweet and decorative White House ornament, they were plain out of luck. She could only be herself—complicated, emotional, and fascinating.

Born in 1818 in Lexington, Kentucky, Mary was the fourth of seven children. Her parents, Robert and Eliza Todd, were wealthy blue bloods (upper-class aristocrats) who often entertained visiting generals, governors, and senators. Vivacious and affectionate, Mary was a favorite among the guests.

The Todds' sprawling fourteen-room house in Lexington ran smoothly thanks to several slaves. When she was small, Mary thought nothing of mammies and maid servants meeting all of her needs. Yet as Mary grew older, she began to question the morality of slavery. She talked to her father about it, and he said: "Someday the peculiar institution will die out, but the time isn't right." Not satisfied with that answer, Mary developed her own views. Later, when she found out that a household slave was hiding runaways, Mary didn't tell a soul.

Probably Mary depended greatly on the kindness of slave women who cared for her, for when Mary was just 7 years old, her own mother died. This tore Mary up inside, and things got worse when her father remarried a woman named Elizabeth Humphries. Mary resented her stepmother terribly, then felt shunted aside when nine stepbrothers and stepsisters came along.

Attendance at a fancy private school helped distract Mary from her unhappy home life. From ages 8 to 17, she studied dancing, literature, and French (which she loved and spoke like a native). After she left school, Mary moved to her married sister's home in Springfield, Illinois, and used her skills to entertain potential husbands.

Petite and lively, Mary could flutter a fan and bat her wide blue eyes with the best of them, so she was quite popular in Springfield's lively party scene. A special talent for telling wonderful stories drew laughing clusters of young people. "Mary," one man commented, "can make a bishop forget his prayers."

Mary also had a strong interest in politics and public affairs, which led to lively discussions with the young lawyers, planters, and politicians. Some in her social set whispered that she would endanger her health with so much thinking. Others admired her quick intelligence. One of those men was the up-and-coming Illinois lawyer and politician Stephen Douglas, who proposed marriage. When Mary turned him down, the cheeky young man reportedly told her she had thrown away her best chance to "rule in the White House." Mary paid him no heed, however, and accepted the attentions of Abraham Lincoln instead.

Legend has it that Abraham Lincoln, a gangly 30-year-old lawyer from Kentucky, met Mary at a dance. He walked up to her and said: "Miss Todd, I'm Abe Lincoln, and I want to dance with you in the worst way." And, they say, that's just what he did—stepping all over her dancing slippers!

Abe Lincoln was poor and pretty funny-looking. He was raised in a little log house and had worked as a blacksmith before becoming a lawyer, moving to Illinois, and getting elected to the state legislature. Everyone expected the high-society Mary Todd to marry someone sophisticated, wealthy, and well connected, not a hayseed like Abe Lincoln. Family and friends suggested she come to her senses, but Mary was deeply drawn to Abe's gentle ways, brilliant mind, and kind soul. They'd both lost their mothers when they were young and understood each other's loneliness. Soon they fell deeply in love.

Knowing her family would object, Mary met Abe secretly for a long time. Then, in November 1842, she informed her sister that they planned to marry right away, with or without family approval. The next day, a simple ceremony was held with thirty friends and relatives attending. A week later, Abe Lincoln wrote to a friend: "Nothing new here, except my marrying, which to me is a matter of profound wonder."

After the wedding, Mary settled with her husband in a single room in a boardinghouse. Right away, the couple began having children, four sons in all—Robert in 1843, Edward in 1846, William in 1850, and Thomas (called Tad because his head was big like a tadpole's) in 1853. The growing family soon moved to a small cottage, then a larger house. Work as a lawyer filled Abe's days, and housework and chores filled Mary's.

Because her husband was on the road a lot and made only a modest income, Mary had a tough time. The once-pampered belle of the ball had no servants, so the chores—from child care and wood chopping to laundry and sewing—were hers alone. After caring for her young sons all day, Mary was very lonely for adult company. When Abe came home in the evening or from a trip, Mary fairly pounced on him for news of politics, law, and society. In fact, Mary grew increasingly interested in Abe's career and was determined to help him climb the political ladder of success.

In 1846, Abe did climb a step higher. He was elected an Illinois representative to the U.S. Congress. Mary was overjoyed and bragged to her family: "One day, he'll be president. You'll see." They thought Mary was batty, but, of course, she was proven right.

Disappointment soon followed on the heels of victory, however, for Abe's first stint in Washington lasted only one term. He did not win the next election, because he took an unpopular stance by opposing slavery in the western territories. Mary agreed with Abe's position but was very upset about his fall from grace. He refused to discuss his feelings with her, though, and Mary complained to a friend: "The more he feels, the less he shows."

Mary lost some of her fight in 1849, when the Lincolns' young son, Eddie, died (of either diphtheria or tuberculosis). Joining the Presbyterian Church provided Mary with some comfort, though, as did caring for the rest of her sons. In the meantime, Abe left politics alone for a while and established himself as a highly respected lawyer.

The introduction of the Kansas-Nebraska Act of 1854 (which would have let voters in new western states decide whether to allow slavery) in Congress propelled Abe back into politics, and Mary approved wholeheartedly. Lincoln's old rival for Mary's affections, the Democratic congressman from Illinois Stephen Douglas, introduced the law, so Lincoln decided to try and take his seat in Congress. In 1858, Lincoln was nominated by the Illinois Republican Party to run against Douglas for Congress.

Seven famous debates between the two candidates attracted huge crowds and the national press. Mary campaigned tirelessly, too, telling everyone she encountered that Stephen Douglas was "a very little giant beside my tall Kentuckian." Despite Mary's championing of her husband, Abe lost the election. Mary was crushed, as was Abe. "I now sink out of view, and shall be forgotten," the future president wrote.

Mary and Abe weren't out of view for long, however. The Republicans decided they'd found their candidate for president and in 1860 asked Abe to run against his old opponent, Stephen A. Douglas. Abe agreed, and Mary was his cheerleader again. In fact, Lincoln liked to tell journalists that Mary had always insisted he was going to be President some day.

When Abe emerged victorious on Election Day, November 6, 1860, he did something that showed his great love for Mary. A crowd waited to greet him outside his window, and his advisers said: "Go forth, Mr. President." But Abe Lincoln merely gave them a weary smile and put on his hat. "Gentlemen, there is a little lady at home who would like to hear this news," he said, then he slipped out a side door and ambled home. "Mary, Mary," he shouted from the door, "we are elected."

Although thrilled that her husband won the presidency, Mary soon discovered that life as a first lady was no picnic. Almost from day one, she worried about Abe's safety, for on the train trip to Washington, crowds rushed him at every station. Even scarier, Southerners tried to stop the train and kidnap the president. Mary and the children had to travel on alone, while Abe and his entourage slipped quietly into Washington on another route.

After that dreadful scare, Mary was a bundle of nerves. But by March 1861, the Lincoln family was soon safely settled in the White House. Abe immediately was caught up in preparing for war (seven states

WOMEN MILITARY ADVISERS

During the Civil War, many women advised, coached, and supported powerful men. Along with his wife, Abe Lincoln turned to Anna Carroll, the daughter of a former governor of Maryland, for advice and assistance. In the fall of 1861, Abe sent Anna to scout out the West to determine whether the Union should go down the Mississippi River and directly attack the Confederates. Anna studied maps, interviewed military leaders, and inspected forts, then reported to Lincoln that the Union should instead attack the rebels via the Cumberland and Tennessee Rivers. (Years later, Ulysses S. Grant launched that very campaign.)

MARY CHESNUT.

Mary Boykin Chesnut of South Carolina also advised her Confederate brigadier general husband, James. The South was hurting because the top brass wouldn't cooperate, she insisted. "You are abusing each other as fiercely as we ever abused Yankees," she told her husband. "That's no way to win a war." The detailed diary Mary kept during the war was published in 1981 by Yale University Press as *Mary Chesnut's Civil War*. The book is so dense with information about Southern wartime history that it won the 1982 Pulitzer Prize.

had already left the Union—South Carolina, Mississippi, Florida, Alabama, Georgia, Louisiana, and Texas—and formed the Confederate States of America), and Mary threw herself into helping the first wounded who staggered into the city. White House servants were put to work assembling care packages of food and flowers, which Mary herself delivered to the hospitals. Mary slipped into the hospitals without fanfare and sat quietly with the wounded soldiers, reading and talking to them. Relief organizations for runaway slaves arriving from the South also benefited from Mary's support.

Because Mary didn't call attention to her charitable deeds, no reporters wrote about them. That was too bad, for the public never knew about Mary's generous nature. What the public did soon know about, however, was her tendency to overspend. This first began when Mary took stock of her new home: the White House. Mary found a royal

---

ELIZABETH KLECKLEY

Right before Abe Lincoln's inauguration on March 2, 1861, the unthinkable happened. Mary Todd Lincoln spilled coffee on her gown. Frantic, she asked for help from Elizabeth Kleckley, a former slave working as a dressmaker in Washington. Before the war, Elizabeth had worked for the Confederate first lady Varina Davis (see chapter 12), too. With lightning speed and great skill, Elizabeth made Mary a gorgeous new dress. After that, the first lady and Elizabeth became close friends.

Along with working as a seamstress, Elizabeth founded and was president of the Contraband Relief Association. In this context, *contraband* meant runaway slaves, and the thousands who flocked to the capital desperately needed food, shelter, and jobs. Mary Lincoln provided start-up funds for the organization, as did the abolitionist Frederick Douglass.

The friendship ended abruptly when, in 1868, Elizabeth wrote a tell-all book: *Behind the Scenes: Thirty Years a Slave and Four in the White House.* The book wasn't critical of the Lincolns, but it had private information in it. Mary was deeply hurt and never spoke to her friend again.

mess—threadbare furniture, peeling paint, moldy carpets, freezing rooms, and worse. So Mary informed Congress this wouldn't do for the nation's executive mansion, and she needed funds for remodeling. Because there was a costly war going on, Congress grumbled, but in the end decided Mary was right and granted the funds.

Mary had a field day gussying up the White House. She had workers install gas lights and central heating, and replace the wallpaper, carpets, curtains, dishes, and furniture. Mary had good taste, too, and really worked wonders, but she also went over budget, which earned her some major enemies.

One reason Mary cared so much about the renovation of the White House was that she longed to be accepted by the elite of Washington high society and thought they would delight in such elegance. However, the new mansion didn't seem to impress high-class Washington ladies at all. In fact, many of the reigning ladies of Washington seemed determined to see Mary as a frumpy country girl.

Mary's unpopularity stemmed partly from her negative publicity and partly from having family members who sided with the Confederacy. (The Todd family was divided between Northern and Southern supporters, and Mary's Confederate soldier brother, Sam, was killed in the Battle of Shiloh.) Some people even spread gossip that Mary was a spy for the South, which was completely unfounded. In fact, Mary opposed slavery more than her husband did, and she was deeply loyal to the Union.

Determined to be a good first lady, Mary took a firm interest in the workings of government and didn't hesitate to tell her husband when she believed generals and other officials were doing a poor job (often she was right, too). Mary also didn't hesitate to lobby her husband for government appointments, which also made her unpopular. Today, being so opinionated might be considered a strength, but a journalist of the time saw it this way: "She meddles not only with the distribution of minor offices, but even with the assignment of places in the Cabinet. Moreover, she allows herself to be approached, and continuously surrounded by, a common set of men and women, who easily gain a controlling influence over her."

To Mary, such criticism cut like a knife and made her even more determined to gain approval. One way she did this was to switch her focus from remodeling to fashion. Mary pored over *Godey's Lady's Book* for the latest tips. Then she traveled to New York to shop until she dropped. "I must dress in costly materials, for the people scrutinize every article that I wear with critical curiosity," the increasingly insecure Mary said.

Wanting to be fashionable and liked doesn't seem so terrible, but even shopping for clothes got Mary into hot water. Because she feared Abe would disapprove of how much she spent, Mary kept it from him. But because she had little money of her own, she'd bought the finery on credit; and when the bills came, she couldn't pay! Secretly, Mary asked friends to loan her money, and the press found out about it. The entire thing became a huge embarrassment for Abe and Mary both.

The humiliating publicity mortified Mary, but it was nothing compared to the grief that hit her in 1862 when 12-year-old Willie Lincoln died (of a stomach ailment then only referred to as bilious fever). When Mary didn't entertain for nearly a year, some people thought that she'd finally gone off the deep end.

Oddly enough, no one jumped all over Mary when—to try to talk to Willie—she began holding séances (attempts to contact the souls of the dead) in the Red Room. The media reported on it but not in a critical way. Séances were all the rage in the mid-nineteenth century. Mary never did hear Willie "speak through" one of the mediums who led the séances she attended. Still, Mary was comforted by vague spirit remarks that Willie was happy in heaven. The mediums also said vague things about Abe having a "shadow hanging over him." And once a medium said Abe's top advisers were plotting against him and should be fired! A couple of times, Abe attended the séances, too, but it's not clear whether he was interested or trying to keep an eye on Mary. One of the few remarks Abe did make about the séances also had to do with his top advisers. The spirits' squabbling voices, Abe said, reminded him of his cabinet!

Today Mary might be labeled troubled, difficult, or maybe just stressed out. (Her many biographers certainly have had different ideas about her state of mind.) But at the time, many people clearly thought Mary was going crazy. This created problems for Abe Lincoln, just when he needed them the least. Yet Abe loved Mary and was deeply loyal to her. At a White House reception, he told a friend: "My wife is as handsome as when she was a girl and I fell in love with her; and what is more, I have never fallen out."

The love of Abe Lincoln's life saw him win a second term as president in 1864. She witnessed the Union victories at Vicksburg and Gettysburg, and she fervently thanked God at the war's end. Mary began spending more time with Abe again, feeling more relaxed and secure. The couple went for a carriage ride into the country and planned an evening at Ford's Theater. Both looked forward to seeing a performance of the hit British comedy *Our American Cousin.* Sadly, that evening at the theater was Abe Lincoln's last.

On the evening of April 14, 1865, the Lincolns shared box seats with young friends, Major Henry Rathbone and Miss Clara Harris. Mary, looking happy and pretty in a striped silk dress, held hands with Abe, and at 10:15 leaned toward him and teased: "What will people think of my hanging on to you so?" Abe replied, "They won't think anything about it." A moment later, the assassin John Wilkes Booth shot Abe Lincoln in the head, then stabbed Major Rathbone and jumped 11 feet to the stage. As Booth escaped from the theater, Mary screamed, clutched her husband, and said to the first doctor who arrived: "Oh, Doctor, is he dead? Can he recover? Will you take charge of him? Oh, my dear husband!"

Abe Lincoln lasted through the night but died early the next morning. Mary's grief was so intense that she wasn't well enough to attend the funeral. Just as soon as she was well enough to travel, Mary left "the dreadful house." With her surviving sons, Robert and Tad, she resettled in Chicago.

Although Mary was deeply depressed, she recovered enough to lobby the government for a pension and got it—the first ever for a first lady. Mary's hard times continued, though, for in 1871 Tad died of pneumonia, then Mary's surviving son, Robert, had her committed to a men-

MARY SURRATT

Mary Surratt, a Southern sympathizer accused of helping the assassin John Wilkes Booth, became the first American woman to be executed by the federal government. Mary owned the boardinghouse where John Wilkes Booth stayed before shooting the president. After the assassination, Mary (along with seven men) was arrested and charged with conspiracy.

Until the moment of her death, Mary Surratt claimed innocence, but the testimony of a tenant at her boardinghouse convicted her. The tenant said that Mary gave binoculars and rifles to Booth on the night of the assassination. Was he telling the truth? Did Mary Surratt deserve to die? Historians today aren't sure, but back then authorities were convinced.

Unfortunately for Mary, if she'd been tried a year later, she might have gone free. After her hanging, the Supreme Court ruled that a military court had no jurisdiction over civilians. When a civilian court later tried Mary's son on similar charges, he was acquitted.

MARY SURRATT.

tal institution. Mary may truly have been dangerously depressed, as Robert claimed. Or Robert, who was running for political office, may have found Mary to be an embarrassment to have around. No one can say for sure, but one thing is certain: Mary considered herself perfectly sane and was furious with her son. During her year in the hospital, Mary went to court, challenged the ruling that she was insane, and won. The judge declared Mary "of sound mind" and set her free.

After her release, Mary moved to France, leaving behind her only surviving child, her country, and her damaged reputation. Only after developing kidney problems did Mary return to live with her sister in Springfield, Illinois, where she died in 1882. At her death, Mary still wore the wedding ring Abe Lincoln had given her decades earlier. Inside it an inscription read: "Love is Eternal. A. Lincoln."

≋☆≋☆≋☆≋☆≋☆≋☆≋☆

Varina Howell Davis

(1 8 2 6 – 1 9 0 6)

Varina Howell Davis, the wife of Jefferson Davis and the first lady of the Confederacy, peppered her politics with Southern charm and stood by her man through thick and thin.

Varina was born in 1826 into a wealthy Natchez, Mississippi, family. Although her family was among the richest in the South, Varina had a strike against her. While her mother, Margaret, came from a leading Southern clan, her father was a New Jersey Yankee. In fact, Varina's grandfather, Richard Howell, was New Jersey's eight-term governor.

Margaret Howell did her best to help Varina overcome this handicap by training her to be the perfect Southern belle. If it hadn't been for the Northern tutors her father hired, her mother would have succeeded completely. Southern girls were expected to ignore the wide world and be terribly demure, but Varina's father and tutors made sure she knew her history and politics. In fact, Varina came to be passionate about public affairs—a trait that might have earned her a reputation for being a bluestocking. Varina also had another trait, however: She kept her smarts under wraps when she was with people who couldn't handle them.

≋☆≋☆≋☆≋☆≋☆≋☆≋☆≋☆≋☆≋☆≋☆≋☆≋☆

THE BLUESTOCKINGS

A woman was called a bluestocking if she had intellectual interests—or pretended to have them. In the mid-1700s, some English ladies had a wild and crazy idea. They would give up card playing and take up thinking! The group held discussions and invited learned men to speak on different subjects. One scholar, named Stillingfleet, said he'd be honored to address the group, but he was too poor to own a pair of black silk stockings. The women told him not to worry—his blue homespun stockings were just fine. Society dubbed the group the Blue Stocking Society, probably hoping the silly name would nip these women's desire to learn in the bud.

★≋★≋★≋★≋★≋★≋★≋★≋★≋★≋★≋★≋★≋★≋★≋

When Varina was 17, it was time to think about marriage. Her father had a particular man in mind—Jefferson Davis, a longtime friend. The handsome widower and Mississippi senator had land, power, and prestige. It didn't matter at all that Jefferson had been married once already (his first wife died of malaria only a few months after their marriage) and was eighteen years older than Varina. Like many upper-crust Southern parents, the Howells believed older men made steadier husbands.

Varina's father sent her on an extended visit to a Louisiana plantation, The Hurricane, owned by Jefferson Davis's brother, Joseph. Every day Jefferson rode his horse over to visit. At first, it seemed the extended blind date was a flop. To her mother, Varina wrote: "Why he's nearly as old as you are!" Jefferson's wild country boy streak—he hunted bear and wrestled alligators for fun—also shocked Varina, but what bothered her most was his strong-mindedness. "He takes it for granted that everybody agrees with him when he expresses an opinion, which offends me," Varina complained.

In a few weeks, however, Varina had forgotten all about these concerns. In spite of his age and wild streak, Jefferson was very much the elegant Southern gent, which Varina admired. Also, Jefferson came to respect Varina's ideas and opinions. Together the couple cantered on horseback across fields, read books aloud to each other, and discussed history, philosophy, and politics. In fact, the match seemed made in heaven, except for one problem Varina couldn't at first get past: Jefferson had joined the new, upstart Democratic Party.

Varina was very loyal to her own Federalist (or Whig) Party, so to her this political difference was a big deal. She scurried home and fretted for weeks about accepting a Democrat as a husband. Finally, love conquered politics, and a lavish wedding was planned. However, because Varina fell ill with "an attack of fever," the wedding was postponed until February 26, 1845. Then in a quiet ceremony held at The Briers, the Howells' home in Natchez, Varina married Jefferson Davis.

After a romantic honeymoon in New Orleans, Varina settled down at Brierfield, Jefferson Davis's Mississippi estate. War, then politics, soon took Jefferson far away from Varina, though, for he was a man on the move. In 1846, Jefferson resigned his seat in Congress to serve in the Mexican War; then from 1847 to 1851, he went to Washington, D.C., to represent Mississippi in the U.S. Senate. (Later, from 1853 to 1857, he'd be President Franklin Pierce's secretary of war, and he'd again be a U.S. senator from 1857 to 1861.) Varina was deeply lonely. So three years after her marriage, in 1848, she packed her bags and resettled with her husband in the nation's capital.

Varina hadn't wanted to leave her beloved South, but her life among the elite politicians and their wives in the capital turned out to be a hoot. For twelve years, she reigned supreme as an elegant Washington hostess—the beautiful "Mississippi Rose." Being gracious and intelligent made Varina revered by most, although some people thought her a bit "too forward." The gossip mill really churned when she defied convention by gadding about even during her six pregnancies in the 1850s and early 1860s. (Four of Varina and Jefferson's children died young. Their daughter Margaret married and had four children, and Varina, or "Winnie," who was born during the war, became known as the daughter of the Confederacy.)

The late 1850s were particularly eventful years for Varina, for Jefferson assumed a leading role among the Southern senators. In 1860, Jefferson warned that the South would secede if Abraham Lincoln was elected president on November 6. The following January, Varina watched from the Senate gallery as her husband announced that Mississippi had left the Union and that he was resigning his post as senator to join the Confederacy.

By February 1861, the Confederate States of America had elected Jefferson president, and Varina and the children were installed in the Confederate White House in Richmond, the new Confederate capitol. Suddenly, Varina was first lady of the South, and she aimed to live up to her title.

JEFFERSON DAVIS.

Varina, in fact, became a power to be reckoned with. She and her husband discussed every aspect of the war, which the cabinet members and generals knew. They said she was "the power behind the throne," so it was wise to keep on her good side. The brass had plenty of opportunities to be close to Varina, too, for she entertained often and lavishly. Remarkably, Varina even managed to get ingredients for plum pudding at Christmastime. Such extravagance peeved Richmond folks, who were barely surviving on cornmeal mush and apples from local orchards. "How dare she, when the rest of Richmond starves?" some folks muttered.

Being the lady of the mansion was expected of Varina, however, and it may have helped her forget her own mounting troubles. When 5-year-old Joseph Davis fell off a balcony of the Confederate White House and died in 1864, Varina had no heart for entertaining. Plus, Jefferson was ill and depressed often, as well as in constant danger of being assassinated. Constant fear of attack by Union forces also created a fearful environment.

By March 1865, that attack was certain and expected any day, so Jefferson handed Varina a pistol and told her to go to Greensboro, North Carolina, and wait for him there. "But I do not expect to survive," he added. To raise money for life in exile, Varina sold her silver, china, carriage horses, clothing, and books. She used her contacts to get the Confederate money converted to $8,000 in gold, which she kept close to her in the wagon. Then, children in tow, on March 27 she left for North Carolina.

A few days later, Jefferson followed, and on the way to meet Varina, he learned that Richmond was captured and General Robert E. Lee had surrendered at Appomattox Court House. Despite this, Jefferson hoped

HUNGRY WOMEN

By 1863, most Southerners were very hungry; some were even starving. No food came into the ports, for Union gunboats kept all trade ships from getting in or out of Southern harbors. Local food was scarce, too, and prices had gone through the roof. Even people in grand plantation manors ate corn bread with bacon drippings for breakfast.

Probably more than anything, Southerners missed bread and coffee. Since flour was scarce, they switched to corn bread. Since coffee was nearly impossible to get, they made substitute brews out of everything from dried peanuts and watermelon seeds to vegetables. Neither was very pleasing, so when merchants did manage to import a bit of flour or coffee, mobs of women flocked to their stores.

Some merchants who did manage to get quantities of flour, coffee, and other scarce goods hid them away. Then they'd put dribs and drabs out to sell when they knew customers were desperate enough to pay a small fortune. When Southern women got wind of such hoarding and price gouging, they got wickedly angry. Sometimes they even marched, protested, and rioted.

In Richmond, women armed with hatchets and sticks swarmed through the streets stealing from stores and shouting: "Bread, bread, bread." Things got so out of control that the troops were called out. The soldiers were set to open fire when President Davis arrived and quieted things down. "If you go home peacefully, I'll see that you get food," he said.

In her diary, one girl wrote: "We celebrated our right to live; we are starving. There is little enough to give after the government has taken our men."

to get to Texas and keep fighting from there. On April 15 (the day Abe Lincoln was shot), Jefferson reached Greensboro, North Carolina, to find his family had gone on ahead and was waiting for him in Dublin, Georgia. There, on May 6, the family reunited, but Georgia turned out to be the end of the line. On May 10, the Davis family woke to find Union cavalry officers on horseback, galloping toward their tents, yelling like demons.

Terrified that her husband would be killed, Varina pleaded with him to don a disguise and escape. In the tent, she draped her own wide cloak around him and a woman's shawl over his head. Then she thrust a bucket into a female servant's hand and ordered her to walk with her husband toward a distant well.

The disguise seemed to work, at first. But the cloak didn't cover Jefferson's spurred boots. An eagle-eyed Union soldier noticed the spurs, pointed his gun right at Jefferson's head, and shouted: "Halt." Jefferson turned, beginning to draw his sword, and Varina knew he wanted to die fighting. Quickly, she dashed out of the tent and threw herself between her husband and the gun-wielding officer. "It's a good thing you didn't resist arrest," the officer growled. "We would have made bloody work of the whole party."

The prisoners were hauled to Union headquarters in Macon, Georgia, and thrown in prison. Varina was released shortly afterward, but her husband was cuffed in irons, charged with treason, and imprisoned at Fort Monroe in Virginia. After taking her children to her parents, who were in exile in Canada, Varina returned to Virginia to try to free her husband. Varina lobbied officials to set her husband free (and for permission to visit him, which wasn't given until a year after the capture). Meanwhile, gossip about Jefferson Davis fleeing arrest in women's clothing spread like wildfire. Edwin Stanton, the secretary of war, was delighted with the tale, for it was a perfect way to humiliate the defeated rebels. Stanton collected eyewitness testimony about the escape and gave it to the Northern newspapers, which exaggerated the facts.

The Union press had a field day, especially political cartoonists who

drew a cowardly Jefferson Davis skulking away in a hoop skirt and bonnet. Jefferson Davis took his fall from grace hard, plus the cold and damp of prison made him weak and ill. When Varina finally did get permission to visit, in May 1866, Jefferson was so depressed and weak that he couldn't rise. Varina held him in her arms and refused to leave until a doctor was called in to treat him.

Jefferson Davis was very lucky to have Varina on his side, for her two years of relentless lobbying won his release in 1867. The family spent a few years in Canada, then returned to the South to stay with friends. Together the couple endured the deaths of their sons William (from diphtheria in 1872) and Jefferson Jr. (from yellow fever in 1878). In 1881, friends willed the couple a Biloxi, Mississippi, estate called Beauvoir. There Jefferson Davis wrote and Varina edited *The Rise and Fall of the Confederate Government,* published in 1881.

Eight years later, Varina's daughter, Winnie, and her husband, Jefferson, died within months of each other. For two days, Jefferson's body was displayed at the New Orleans Memorial Hall, a museum founded in 1891 by Confederate veterans. More than 60,000 people walked by his coffin to pay their respects. After all that Southern patriotism, what the widowed Varina did next is surprising. She told friends she'd always wanted to live in New York City—and away she went. In the city, she wrote some magazine articles and a book, *Jefferson Davis: A Memoir by His Wife.* At her death in 1906, the Beauvoir estate went to the state of Mississippi to be used as a Confederate veteran's home. Varina also left some precious mementos—including her husband's top hat, Bible, and a crown of thorns given to him by Pope Pius IX—to the New Orleans Memorial Hall.

Albe, Helen. *Susan B. Anthony: Champion of Women's Rights* (Childhood of Famous Americans Series). New York, Aladdin Paperbacks, 1896.

Beller, Susan Provost. *Confederate Ladies of Richmond.* New York, Twenty First Century Books, 1999.

Bolotin, Norman, Angela Herb, and Brian C. Pohanka. *For Home and Country: A Civil War Scrapbook.* Holmen, Wisconsin, Lodestar, 1994.

Brackett, Virginia. *John Brown: Abolitionist* (Famous Figures of the Civil War Era). New York, Chelsea House, 2001.

Brindell Fraden, Dennis. *Bound for the North Star: True Stories of Fugitive Slaves.* New York, Clarion Books, 2000.

Chang, Ina. *A Separate Battle: Women and the Civil War.* New York, Puffin, 1996.

Clinton, Catherine. *Scholastic Encyclopedia of the Civil War.* New York, Scholastic Trade, 1999.

Copeland, Peter F. *The Story of the Underground Railroad.* Mineola, New York, Dover Publications, 2000.

Denenberg, Barry. *When Will This Cruel War Be Over?: The Civil War Diary of Emma Simpson, Gordonsville, Virginia, 1864* (Dear America). New York, Scholastic Trade, 1996.

Egger-Bovet, Howard, and Marlene Smith-Baranzini. *USKids History: Book of the American Civil War.* Boston, Little, Brown, 1998.

Freedman, Russell. *Lincoln: A Photobiography.* New York, Clarion Books, 1987.

Fritz, Jean. *Harriet Beecher Stowe and the Beecher Preachers.* Paper Star, 1998.

Fritz, Jean. *Stonewall.* New York, Putnam, 1979.

Gorrell, Gena K. *Heart and Soul: The Story of Florence Nightingale.* Plattsburgh, New York, Tundra Books, 2000.

Hakim, Joy. *War. Terrible War* (History of Us, Book 6). New York, Oxford University Press Childrens Books, 1999.

Hesse, Karen. *A Light in the Storm: The Civil War Diary of Amelia Martin, Fenwick Island, Delaware, 1861* (Dear America). New York, Scholastic Trade, 1999.

King, David. *Civil War Days: Discover the Past with Exciting Projects, Games, Activities, and Recipes.* New York, John Wiley, 1999.

Levine, Ellen. *If You Traveled on the Underground Railroad.* New York, Scholastic Trade, 1993.

Lutz, Norma Jean, and Schlesinger, Arthur M., Jr. *Frederick Douglass: Abolitionist and Author* (Famous Figures of the Civil War Era). New York, Chelsea House, 2001.

McCurdy, Michael, ed. *Escape from Slavery: The Boyhood of Frederick Douglass in His Own Words.* New York, Alfred A. Knopf, 1994.

McGovern, Ann. *Wanted Dead or Alive: The True Story of Harriet Tubman.* New York, Scholastic Trade, 1991.

McKissack, Patricia C. and Frederick McKissack. *Sojourner Truth: Ain't I a Woman?* New York, Scholastic Trade, 1994

Meigs, Cornelia Lynde. *Invincible Louisa: The Story of the Author of Little Women.* Boston, Little Brown & Co, 1968.

Moore, Kay. *If You Lived at the Time of the Civil War.* New York, Scholastic Trade, 1994.

Murphy, Jim. *The Boys' War.* New York, Clarion Books, 1990.

Rappaport, Doreen. *Escape from Slavery: Five Journeys to Freedom.* New York, HarperCollins, 1999.

Ray, Delia. *A Nation Torn: The Story of How the Civil War Began* (Young Readers' History of the Civil War). New York, Puffin, 1996.

Reit, Seymour. *Lines: The Incredible Story of Emma Edmonds, Civil War Spy* (Great Episodes). Fairbanks, Alaska, Gulliver Books, August 2001.

Rinaldi, Ann. *Girl in Blue.* New York, Scholastic Trade, 2001.

Rockwell, Anne F. *Only Passing Through: The Story of Sojourner Truth.* New York, Knopf, 2000.

Sandler, Martin W. *Civil War* (Library of Congress Books). New York, HarperCollins Juvenile Books, 1996.

Santow, Dan. *Mary Todd Lincoln: 1818–1882* (Encyclopedia of First Ladies). Chicago, Children's Press, 1999.

Sinnott, Susan. *Welcome to Addy's World, 1864: Growing Up During America's Civil War* (American Collection). Middleton, Wisconsin, Pleasant Company Publications, 1999.

Sneden, Robert Knox. *Images from the Storm: 300 Civil War Images.* New York, Free Press, 2001.

Stanchak, John E. *Eyewitness: Civil War.* New York/London, DK, 2000.

Stevenson, Augusta. *Clara Barton, Founder of the American Red Cross* (The Childhood of Famous Americans Series). New York, Aladdin Paperbacks, 1986.

Sullivan, George. *The Day the Women Got the Vote: A Photo History of the Women's Rights Movement.* New York, Scholastic Paperbacks, 1994.

Taylor, M. W. *Harriet Tubman* (Black Americans of Achievement). New York, Chelsea House, 1991.

Wisler, Clifton, G. *When Johnny Went Marching Home: Young Americans Fight the Civil War.* New York, HarperCollins Children's Books, 2001.

Page 8: Photograph used courtesy of Louisa May Alcott Memorial Association; pages 20 and 23: property of Seneca Falls Historical Society; pages 27, 34, 35, 48, 58, 62, 68, and 102: Library of Congress; page 29: courtesy of the American Textile History Museum-Lowell, Mass.; page 40: courtesy Ohio Historical Society; pages 44, 59, and 115: courtesy National Archives; page 50: Massachusetts Commandery, Military Order of the Loyal Legion and the U.S. Army Military History Institute; pages 53, 78, 87, 91, and 112: National Portrait Gallery, Smithsonian Institution/Art Resource, N.Y.; page 72: Chicago Historical Society; page 88: courtesy of PictureHistory; page 96: courtesy State Archives Michigan; page 106: Art Resource, N.Y.; page 111: courtesy Surratt House Museum.

Myra Colby Bradwell. Myra's marriage to the lawyer James B. Bradwell inspired her interest in the field of law. In 1868, she established and edited the weekly *Chicago Legal News,* which she ran until her death in 1894. In 1869, Myra helped organize Chicago's first woman suffrage convention, and that same year she passed the qualifying bar exam for lawyers. But when Myra applied to the Illinois Supreme Court for permission to practice law, she was refused. That decision was upheld by the U.S. Supreme Court in May 1873. Not until 1892, two years before Myra's death, did the Illinois Supreme Court reverse its decision.

Mary Shadd Cary. After fleeing to Canada on the Underground Railroad, the ex-slave published *The Provincial Freemen* "to acquaint the white citizens with the noble deeds and heroism of the colored American." After marrying in 1856, she opened an integrated school in Canada, and later ran a school in Delaware. In 1863, the army appointed her as a recruiter, and she enlisted black volunteers in Indiana. After the war, she enrolled in Howard University Law Department and became a lawyer in 1883.

Lydia Francis Childs. The author, editor, and abolitionist Lydia Francis Child wrote "An Appeal in Favor of That Class of Americans Called Africans" in 1833, which related the history of slavery and prejudice against blacks. Lydia also edited publications, harbored fugitive slaves, transcribed the memories of ex-slaves, and wrote books about the struggles of Native Americans.

Jane Croly. After the New York Press Club refused to admit women to a reception for the British author Charles Dickens, Jane Croly (an editor at *New York World*) formed the Sorosis Club for professional women in 1868. She also convened a national convention of women's clubs in 1889, which formed the General Federation of Women's Clubs.

Abigail Scott Duniway. Along with writing a memoir about her family's 2,400-mile journey to Oregon in 1852, Abigail raised six children, taught school, and published for *The New Northwest,* a weekly newspaper dedicated to the cause of women's rights. When Susan B. Anthony toured the Pacific Northwest in

1871, Abigail was by her side. She also founded the Oregon Equal Suffrage Association, which in 1883 won the vote for women in the Washington Territory.

Margaret Fuller. One of America's first female journalists, Margaret joined the *New York Tribune* as a literary critic in the 1840s. She also served as a European correspondent. In 1845, she wrote the book *Woman in the Nineteenth Century.* Shortly afterward, she married an Italian revolutionary, Giovanni Angelo Ossoli, and had a son. In 1850, the entire family died at sea while returning to America from Italy.

Rebecca Gratz. A leader in Philadelphia's Jewish community, Rebecca dedicated her life to helping the less fortunate. While raising several of her deceased sister's children, she organized the Female Association for the Relief of Women and Children of Reduced Circumstances, the Philadelphia Orphan Asylum, the Female Hebrew Benevolent Society, the Jewish Foster Home and Orphan Asylum, and the Hebrew Sunday School Society.

Anna Jarvis. The woman who inspired Mother's Day nursed both Confederate and Union wounded who fought near her central West Virginia home. After the war, Anna saw how much bitterness remained between the two sides. To help people heal, she organized a Mothers' Friendship Day picnic. On that day, which would become an annual event for several years, mothers in the community brought their children and grandchildren—no matter what their politics. When Anna died in 1905, her daughter, also named Anna Jarvis, lobbied the government to create a national holiday called Mother's Day. The holiday was established in 1914.

Mary Mahoney. The first African American woman to become a trained nurse was born in Massachusetts and graduated in 1879 from the New England Hospital for Women and Children (founded during the Civil War). It was a tough course, for of the eighteen women who started the program, only four graduated. Mary was active in the American Nurses Association and the movement for women's suffrage.

Maria Martin. The Charleston, South Carolina, artist was a friend and student of John James Audubon, the famous artist and naturalist. She began by painting backgrounds and details for Audubon's watercolor portraits of birds, and later contributed more of the artwork. She was Audubon's only female assistant and also contributed drawings to books by other artists of the day.

Maria Mitchell. The Nantucket, Massachusetts, native learned about the stars from her father, who ran a whaling fleet. From 1836 to 1856, she worked as a librarian, and by night she observed the stars through a telescope. In 1847, she discovered the orbit of a new comet, and the next year she became the first woman elected to the American Academy of Arts and Sciences. In 1865, she became a faculty member at Vassar Female College, in Poughkeepsie, New York, and in 1873, she founded the Association for the Advancement of Women.

Lucretia Coffin Mott. A Quaker minister, women's rights pioneer, and religious reformer, Lucretia raised six children, led abolitionist groups, sheltered runaway slaves, and called for boycotts of goods made by slave labor. In 1848, her remarks opened America's first women's rights convention in Seneca Falls, New York. After the Civil War, Lucretia was elected the first president of the American Equal Rights Association.

Elizabeth Peabody. The Massachusetts educator, publisher, and writer ran schools, promoted public education, opened America's first kindergarten, studied Greek, and befriended the top poets, writers, and thinkers of the time. In 1839, Elizabeth opened a Boston bookstore that became the social club for the intellectual crowd of the city. She also published the intellectuals' books (including Henry David Thoreau's) and sermons.

Lucy Stone. Although she wasn't the first woman to keep her own name after marriage, Lucy made a big public issue of it. So women who followed her example were called "Stoners." In 1847, Lucy graduated from Oberlin College in Ohio, the first college in the United States to accept women (in 1837). Yet even at that hotbed of reform she wasn't allowed to give her own valedictorian speech.

Susie King Taylor. As a slave in Savannah, Georgia, Susie secretly learned to read and write. When Union troops invaded in 1862, Susie and other slaves were moved to Georgia's St. Simon's Island. There she taught in a school for the children of ex-slaves and married Edward King, a sergeant with the black Union troops. Susie followed Edward into the field, working as a laundress, secretary, and nurse. After the war, Susie relocated with her child to Boston because Edward had died. She married Russell L. Taylor and in 1902 wrote *Reminiscences of My Life in Camp: With the U.S. 33rd Colored United States Troops.*